Biobanking Ethics and Regulation in East Asia

This book offers a comprehensive analysis of Malaysia's biobanking landscape, examining the complex intersection of ethics, law, and culture in a rapidly developing healthcare research environment.

Adopting a case-based methodology, this book presents realistic scenarios that mirror dilemmas faced by ethics committees, researchers, and policymakers. Each chapter begins with a hypothetical case study followed by detailed commentary analysing ethical concerns, regulatory gaps, and best practices within Malaysia's unique socio-legal context. By exploring globally relevant topics like informed consent in multicultural settings, religious perspectives on tissue ownership, data privacy in cross-border collaborations, commercialisation of biospecimens, and incidental findings management, this book bridges the gap between academic theory and professional application.

This book will be of interest to scholars of bioethics, medical law, healthcare regulation, and health policy, especially those in Southeast Asia.

Mohammad Firdaus Bin Abdul Aziz is Senior Lecturer and Deputy Dean of Research and Innovation at the Faculty of Law, Universiti Malaya. He obtained his DPhil from the University of Oxford. Currently, he is a co-investigator on a UK Wellcome Trust–funded initiative aimed at establishing a bioethics network in Southeast Asia and a co-investigator on the US National Institute of Health (NIH) Fogarty grant, which focuses on developing a master's program in health research ethics at Universiti Malaya.

Routledge Studies in Asian Law

Constitutional Remedies in Asia
Edited by Po Jen Yap

Philosophy of Law in Korea
Acceptance, Engagement and Social Change
Jeong-Oh Kim, Hak-Tai Kim, Joon-Seok Park, Dong-Ryong Shin

The Law and Regulation of Public Health
Global Perspectives on Hong Kong
Eric C. Ip

State Administrative Law in Indonesia
M. Zaenul Muttaqin

Stem Cell Governance and Ethics
Mohammad Firdaus Bin Abdul Aziz

Law and Justice in Small Island Developing States
Lessons from Niue
Mana Takahashi and Kahealani Sinahemana Hekau

Decodification of the Civil Code of the People's Republic of China
Igor Szpotakowski

Biobanking Ethics and Regulation in East Asia
Lessons from Malaysia
Mohammad Firdaus Bin Abdul Aziz

For more information about this series, please visit: https://www.routledge.com/asianstudies/series/RSIAL

Biobanking Ethics and Regulation in East Asia

Lessons from Malaysia

Mohammad Firdaus Bin Abdul Aziz

Routledge
Taylor & Francis Group
LONDON AND NEW YORK

First published 2027
by Routledge
4 Park Square, Milton Park, Abingdon, Oxon OX14 4RN

and by Routledge
605 Third Avenue, New York, NY 10158

Routledge is an imprint of the Taylor & Francis Group, an informa business

British Library Cataloguing-in-Publication Data
A catalogue record for this book is available from the British Library

ISBN: 978-1-041-25256-6 (hbk)
ISBN: 978-1-041-25244-3 (pbk)
ISBN: 978-1-003-74578-5 (ebk)

DOI: 10.4324/9781003745785

Typeset in Times New Roman
by Apex CoVantage, LLC

In loving memory of my parents,
and to my wife,
for her unwavering support.

Contents

Preface

Biobanks have become critical infrastructures in contemporary biomedical science, enabling discoveries in medicine, genetics, and public health that were previously unimaginable. In Malaysia, the biobanking sector has expanded, driven by both the growing demand for biomedical data and a national commitment to improving healthcare outcomes. Yet, as these repositories of biological materials and associated data grow in scale and influence, they also generate complex ethical and legal questions that extend beyond technical regulation into the social and relational dimensions of research governance.

This book explores these challenges through a series of case studies that illuminate the ethical dilemmas encountered by biobanks, their stakeholders, and the wider community. The intention is not merely to catalogue problems but to foster thoughtful reflection on how institutions can balance scientific progress with respect for individual rights, cultural diversity, and collective societal values. Each chapter presents a realistic scenario followed by analytical commentary, highlighting the ethical and legal tensions that arise within the Malaysian context while drawing insight from international principles and comparative practices.

Biobanks operate at the intersection of healthcare, law, and scientific inquiry, but they are also social institutions sustained by public trust and ongoing relationships with participants. Ethical governance in this field therefore requires more than procedural compliance. It demands stewardship, transparency, and responsiveness to evolving social expectations. Malaysia's legal and regulatory landscape surrounding biobanking continues to develop, and this book seeks to provide both a diagnostic and constructive perspective on how these issues are currently addressed, where gaps remain, and how governance practices may continue to mature.

It is worth highlighting that this book does not seek to prescribe definitive solutions to the ethical and regulatory dilemmas presented. The purpose of the case studies and accompanying analyses is therefore not to provide universal answers. The case studies presented are hypothetical and are designed to provoke analysis rather than replicate specific events. The intention is to cultivate critical reflection, ethical sensitivity, and informed dialogue among stakeholders. Nonetheless, they are informed by real-world concerns but intentionally anonymised and generalised to encourage broader application. It is hoped that through these scenarios, researchers, policymakers, legal practitioners, ethics committees, and biobank professionals will gain clearer insight into the ethical and legal dimensions of biobanking and be better equipped to navigate the responsibilities that accompany scientific advancement.

This work is intended as a practical yet reflective resource for those involved in or affected by biobanking practices. By engaging with these questions, the book contributes to an ongoing conversation about how biomedical innovation can progress alongside principled governance, cultural sensitivity, and relational accountability in Malaysia and beyond.

Mohammad Firdaus Bin Abdul Aziz

Purpose and Scope

The primary purpose of this book is to provide an in-depth analysis of the ethical and legal challenges facing biobanks in Malaysia. By presenting hypothetical case studies and accompanying commentary, the book explores complex issues such as:

- Informed consent – how can biobanks ensure that participants understand the scope of their involvement and the potential uses of their biological samples and data?
- Privacy and confidentiality – what measures should be in place to protect the sensitive personal and health information of participants?
- Commercialisation – how can biobanks balance scientific progress with ethical concerns related to profit-making and the potential exploitation of human resources?
- Return of incidental health findings – should biobanks return unexpected health information to participants, and if so, under what conditions?
- International data sharing – what are the ethical and legal implications of sharing biological data across borders, particularly when laws differ from country to country?

The scope of the book is to address these questions within the Malaysian context while drawing on international principles and best practices. The case studies presented throughout the book offer realistic scenarios that allow readers to explore potential solutions and discuss the broader implications of biobank practices. Through these discussions, the book aims to provide biobank professionals, policymakers, and researchers with guidance in addressing ethical and legal issues in biobanking.

1 Introduction

1.1 Overview

Biobanks have emerged as a cornerstone of modern scientific research, providing invaluable resources for advancing knowledge in medicine, genetics, and public health. By collecting, storing, and sharing human biological samples together with associated data, biobanks enable discoveries that deepen understanding of disease, inform personalised medicine, and strengthen preventive-health strategies. In Malaysia, the growth of the biobanking sector has been particularly notable, supported by national research initiatives and increasing participation in international collaborations. As these repositories become embedded within the country's scientific infrastructure, they also give rise to ethical and legal challenges that require careful, context-sensitive governance.

This book examines these challenges through a structured series of hypothetical case studies situated within the Malaysian socio-legal and cultural environment. The aim is not only to identify areas of regulatory uncertainty or ethical tension, but also to illuminate how biobanking operates as both a scientific and a social institution. Decisions regarding biological materials and personal data are rarely purely technical; they involve questions of autonomy, dignity, fairness, and trust that extend beyond laboratory procedures into broader societal relationships. Ethical legitimacy in biobanking therefore depends as much on relational accountability and institutional stewardship as it does on formal legal compliance.

Each chapter addresses a distinct yet interconnected domain of concern – namely, informed consent, privacy and confidentiality, commercialisation, the management of incidental findings, and international data sharing. These themes are not isolated issues but represent different dimensions of value and responsibility attached to human biological materials. The progression of chapters reflects a movement from individual rights toward collective and cross-border considerations, illustrating how governance challenges expand as research infrastructures grow in scale and complexity.

DOI: 10.4324/9781003745785-1

Malaysia offers a particularly instructive context for examining these dynamics. Its multi-ethnic and multi-religious composition introduces layers of cultural and normative diversity that influence participant expectations, consent practices, and interpretations of fairness. At the same time, Malaysia's regulatory landscape remains evolving rather than static, characterised by a combination of statutory law, ministerial guidelines, institutional ethics oversight, and international soft-law influences. This environment presents both challenges and opportunities – challenges in achieving regulatory coherence, and opportunities for adaptive governance capable of responding to technological and social change.

The hypothetical case-study method adopted in this book serves as an analytical tool rather than a pedagogical exercise alone. These scenarios are designed to simulate real-world tensions, enabling readers to explore ethical reasoning and legal interpretation without the constraints of actual litigation or institutional confidentiality. Through this approach, the book aims to bridge theoretical reflection and practical application, encouraging readers to engage with governance questions not as abstract doctrines but as lived institutional responsibilities.

Ultimately, this work positions biobanks not merely as data repositories or research facilities but as enduring social partnerships between institutions and participants. The discussions that follow seek to demonstrate that ethical biobanking is not achieved through isolated compliance measures but through sustained stewardship, transparent communication, and trust-building practices that evolve alongside scientific progress.

Chapter 1 provides an overview of biobanking in Malaysia, introducing the scientific significance of biobanks, the regulatory frameworks that shape their operation, and the ethical considerations that underpin their legitimacy. This introductory chapter establishes the conceptual and institutional landscape upon which the subsequent analyses are grounded.

Chapter 2 examines informed consent, a cornerstone of ethical biobanking practice. Moving beyond formal documentation, this chapter explores consent as an ongoing communicative process, addressing linguistic, cultural, and contextual challenges in ensuring that participants meaningfully understand their rights, expectations, and the implications of their involvement.

Chapter 3 turns to issues of privacy and confidentiality, focusing on the protection of personal and genetic data within the biobank environment. It analyses Malaysia's data-protection framework alongside ethical concerns surrounding re-identification risks, collective privacy, and the stewardship responsibilities of research institutions.

Chapter 4 addresses the commercialisation of biobanks, highlighting the ethical tension between scientific advancement and economic interests. Through case-based analysis, this chapter explores benefit-sharing, commodification concerns, and the legal implications that arise when public research infrastructures engage with private or profit-oriented entities.

Chapter 5 examines the governance of incidental findings, focusing on the ethical responsibilities of biobanks when unexpected health-related information emerges from research activities. The chapter considers the balance between disclosure, participant welfare, and the right not to know, situating these dilemmas within Malaysia's regulatory and cultural context.

Chapter 6 explores international data sharing and cross-border collaboration, analysing the ethical and legal complexities that arise when biological data and samples move beyond national jurisdiction. Particular attention is given to consent validity, sovereignty, power asymmetry, and the challenges posed by differing national privacy regimes and global research partnerships.

Chapter 7, the concluding chapter, synthesises the ethical, legal, and governance themes developed throughout the book. It reflects on the role of trust, stewardship, and relational accountability in sustaining ethical biobanking practices, and considers Malaysia's evolving trajectory within regional and global biomedical governance.

Through these chapters, the book seeks to provide both theoretical insight and practical guidance for understanding and addressing the ethical and legal dimensions of biobanking. It is intended as a resource for researchers, policymakers, biobank professionals, and ethicists who are committed to fostering responsible and culturally grounded governance in biomedical research.

By the end of this work, readers are invited not only to navigate the complex terrain of biobank regulation in Malaysia and beyond, but also to recognise biobanks as institutions that carry enduring social and relational responsibilities alongside their scientific value.

1.2 The Biobanking Landscape in Malaysia

The biobank landscape in Malaysia has evolved into a significant component of the country's scientific and research infrastructure, contributing to advancements in biomedical science, genomics, personalised medicine, and public health policy. Biobanks in Malaysia operate within a socio-legal and cultural environment shaped by ethnic diversity, varying health burdens, and increasing participation in regional and global research collaborations. Malaysia's multi-ethnic demographic composition, comprising Malays, Chinese, Indians, and numerous Indigenous communities, provides an especially valuable context for genetic and epidemiological studies, enabling comparative analyses that are less readily achievable in more demographically homogeneous populations.

The Malaysian biobanking ecosystem consists of multiple institutional forms, including population-based national cohort biobanks, government-linked research repositories, university-based institutional biobanks, disease-specific research collections, and commercial or private biological storage services. These models differ in their objectives, governance structures, recruitment strategies, and ethical implications. Some are primarily research-oriented and publicly funded, whereas others function within clinical or commercial frameworks. Collectively, they illustrate the pluralistic nature of Malaysia's biomedical research landscape and highlight the need for adaptable governance mechanisms capable of addressing differing operational realities.

1.2.1 The Malaysia Cohort Project

The Malaysia Cohort Project, commonly referred to as *The Malaysian Cohort (TMC)*, represents the most prominent population-based biobank initiative in Malaysia and is frequently cited as a national flagship programme in biomedical research. Established following Cabinet approval in 2005 and operationally anchored at Universiti Kebangsaan Malaysia, the project was conceived as a long-term prospective cohort study aimed at generating a comprehensive biospecimen repository and integrated health database (*The Malaysian Cohort*). Its central objective is to investigate non-communicable diseases (NCDs), including diabetes, cardiovascular diseases, obesity, and metabolic syndromes, while also exploring gene-environment interactions and biomarker discovery for early detection and preventive health strategies.

Recruitment efforts targeted individuals aged between 35 and 70 years across both urban and rural regions, ultimately exceeding the initial target of 100,000 participants. This scale distinguishes TMC from most other Malaysian repositories and positions it as a regional comparative platform within Southeast Asia. The cohort's design emphasises demographic inclusivity and cross-ethnic representation, enabling analysis of health disparities, genetic predispositions, and lifestyle determinants across Malaysia's diverse population groups (Jamal et al., 2015).

Key Features and Goals

COMPREHENSIVE MULTIDIMENSIONAL DATA COLLECTION

Participants undergo detailed baseline assessments that include physical examinations, biochemical analyses, lifestyle questionnaires, and biospecimen collection such as blood, urine, and DNA. These data are digitised and stored within secure research databases, creating a longitudinal dataset capable of supporting multidisciplinary inquiry.

LONGITUDINAL FOLLOW-UP AND PREDICTIVE ANALYTICS

The longitudinal design permits tracking of disease incidence and progression over extended periods. This temporal dimension enables predictive modelling, risk stratification, and evaluation of preventive interventions at both individual and population levels.

ETHNIC AND SOCIO-GEOGRAPHIC DIVERSITY

Malaysia's demographic heterogeneity allows the cohort to generate insights into culturally mediated health behaviours and genetic variability, enhancing the global relevance of its findings.

PUBLIC HEALTH AND POLICY RELEVANCE

Although not a formal policymaking body, the evidence generated by the Malaysian Cohort contributes to national health-planning discourse and informs preventive-health initiatives, particularly in relation to NCD management and screening strategies.

RESEARCH AND IMPACT

Research outputs from the Malaysian Cohort have included epidemiological analyses, genomic association studies, and exploratory pharmacogenomic research. The availability of biospecimens linked with lifestyle and clinical metadata has also supported investigations into environmental exposures, metabolic disorders, and early-stage biomarker identification (Jamal et al., 2015).

1.2.2 Government-Linked and Public Health Research Repositories

In addition to large-scale population cohorts, Malaysia maintains a network of government-linked biological repositories embedded within the public-health research infrastructure, particularly under the Ministry of Health and its National Institutes of Health (NIH) cluster. These repositories are often laboratory-based and decentralised rather than consolidated into a single national "biobank", yet they collectively function as strategic biological archives supporting infectious-disease surveillance, diagnostic research, and outbreak preparedness.

Their operational focus differs from population biobanks in that sample acquisition is frequently linked to clinical encounters, hospital admissions, or targeted surveillance programmes. During periods of public-health emergency, most notably the COVID-19 pandemic, these repositories played a crucial role in pathogen sequencing, vaccine-response studies, and epidemiological modelling. Their importance lies less in cohort size and more in real-time responsiveness and clinical integration, enabling rapid mobilisation of biological data during health crises.

1.2.3 University-Based Institutional Biobanks

University-based institutional biobanks constitute another important dimension of Malaysia's research ecosystem (Vaithilingam et al., 2015; Zain et al., 2013). Typically situated within faculties of medicine, dentistry, pharmacy, or allied health sciences, these repositories are designed to support investigator-initiated studies, postgraduate theses, and collaborative research projects. Unlike national cohort biobanks, institutional repositories are generally **project-specific and grant-driven**, with sample collections linked to defined research protocols rather than continuous open recruitment.

These biobanks perform dual functions. First, they provide logistical and technical infrastructure for laboratory-based research, including specimen storage, sample processing, and data management. Second, they serve as educational platforms, enabling training in laboratory techniques, research ethics, and data stewardship for emerging scientists. Governance is usually exercised through institutional research-ethics committees and internal policy frameworks, embedding ethical oversight within the academic environment itself.

1.2.4 Disease-Specific Research Biobanks

Disease-specific repositories, such as the Malaysian Periodontal Database and Biobank System (Vaithilingam et al., 2015) and Malaysian Oral Cancer Database and Tissue Bank System (Zain et al., 2013), are typically associated with specialist medical centres or hospital departments focusing on oncology, oral health, or other targeted clinical domains. Their defining feature is depth rather than breadth, whereby collections are narrower in scope but richer in clinical annotation. Samples may include tumour tissues, biopsy specimens, blood derivatives, and associated histopathological or imaging records.

These repositories play a pivotal role in translational medicine by bridging laboratory findings with clinical practice. They enable biomarker discovery, therapeutic-response analysis, and precision-medicine initiatives tailored to specific disease populations. Their ethical considerations often revolve around consent for secondary use, return of clinically significant findings, and management of highly sensitive medical information.

1.2.5 Commercial and Private Biobanking Services

Commercial or private biobanking services in Malaysia most commonly operate in the domain of **cord blood (*CryoCord Sdn Bhd*) and stem-cell preservation (*StemLife Berhad*)**, offering long-term storage solutions for families seeking potential future therapeutic options. Unlike research-driven repositories, these entities function under a contractual, fee-based model in which ownership and access rights typically remain with the client.

The commercial nature of these services introduces distinct ethical and regulatory questions, including issues of informed consent, marketing transparency, data ownership, and equitable access. Although they contribute to biomedical preparedness at an individual or family level, their impact on public research is indirect unless collaborative agreements with research institutions are established. Oversight is generally provided through healthcare-facility licensing, laboratory accreditation standards, and general health-law regulations rather than specialised biobank statutes.

Taken together, Malaysia's biobanking landscape reflects a layered and pluralistic ecosystem rather than a singular institutional model. Population-based cohorts, government research archives, academic repositories, disease-specific collections, and private storage services collectively contribute to the nation's biomedical capacity while presenting diverse ethical and legal challenges. As the sector continues to expand, sustained attention to governance harmonisation, participant trust, and culturally grounded ethical oversight will be essential to ensuring that scientific advancement proceeds alongside social responsibility and regulatory clarity.

Because these biobank models differ in funding, sectoral location, and operational purpose, they are governed through different combinations of statutes, ministerial guidance, ethics review pathways, and contractual instruments, making regulatory consistency and public trust especially imperative.

1.3 The Regulatory Framework for the Biobanking Sector in Malaysia

The biobanking sector in Malaysia operates within a hybrid regulatory ecosystem rather than under a single dedicated biobank statute. The existing governance for biobanking activities in Malaysia draws on (i) general legislation relevant to human tissues, personal data, and regulated health services; (ii) national research ethics frameworks and ministry guidance that address ethical concerns surrounding this realm, such as consent, custodianship, access, confidentiality, and transfer practices; and (iii) institutional oversight through research ethics committees and operational governance structures within ministries, universities, hospitals, and where relevant, private healthcare providers.

As shown in Section 1.2, Malaysia's biobanks are diverse in institutional form (governmental, university-based, and private), which means that the regulatory "fit" varies by sector. This is particularly evident in data protection, whereby the PDPA regulates personal data in commercial contexts and does not apply to Federal and State Governments, and this creates different compliance pathways for public-sector versus private-sector biobanks.

1.3.1 Structure of Governance in Practice

In practice, governance of biobanking in Malaysia is typically implemented through a combination of:

- **Ethics review and continuing oversight** by either Research Ethics Committee (REC), Institutional Review Board (IRB), or Independent Ethics Committee processes for research using identifiable samples and/or associated data;
- **Information governance** including policies on de-identification, controlled access, data security, retention/disposal, and accountability roles;
- **Transfer governance** for inter-institutional and cross-border sharing, which is regulated by formal agreements (e.g., MTAs/DTAs) that require the specification of custodianship responsibilities;
- **Sectoral regulation**, where biobanking activities sit within regulated healthcare services (e.g., private hospitals, assisted reproduction, cord blood banking), which introduces quality/safety requirements and ministry approval processes.

1.3.2 Key Regulatory Instruments

Several key legislative and regulatory instruments shape biobanking governance in Malaysia. Importantly, these do not operate as a single unified code, but they function as overlapping "umbrella" instruments supplemented by national guidance and institutional policies.

This section first outlines data-protection rules (PDPA and its amendments) for private-sector biobanking and partnerships, then discusses the Human Tissues Act 1974 as a limited statutory backdrop for human tissue use, followed by MOH guidance and MOH ethics governance mechanisms (NMRR/MREC) that shape public-sector practice. It then highlights sectoral regulation relevant to private healthcare-linked biobanking, including cord blood banking standards, and finally notes key international ethical instruments and Malaysia's advisory bioethics architecture.

(a) Personal Data Protection Act 2010 (PDPA) and the Personal Data Protection (Amendment) Act 2024

The PDPA (Act 709) is Malaysia's primary statute regulating the processing of personal data in commercial transactions ("Personal Data Protection Act", 2010). For biobanking, this matters most where activities are conducted by or via private-sector entities (including private healthcare facilities, commercial research organisations, and private laboratories) and involve personal data processing within the PDPA's commercial scope (Abdul Aziz & Mohd Yusof, 2019).

Core features of the PDPA relevant to biobanking include:

- **Scope limits (sectoral boundary)**
  The PDPA states that it does not apply to the Federal Government and State Governments. This is consequential because many major public research activities and public biobanks are government-linked; nonetheless, MOH guidance notes that government actors must instead follow applicable governmental acts, circulars, regulations, and guidelines when processing personal information.
- **Health data as "sensitive personal data"**
  The PDPA defines "sensitive personal data" to include information about a data subject's physical or mental health or condition, which conceptually captures much of the data handled by clinical and research biobanks.
- **Baseline processing expectations**
  The PDPA sets out Personal Data Protection Principles (including consent, notice/choice, disclosure, security, retention, data integrity, and access), which shape privacy-by-design expectations for PDPA-covered biobanks and their contractors.

From a current perspective, the PDPA must also be read together with recent reforms – namely, the Personal Data Protection (Amendment) Act 2024 (Act A1727) (Royal Assent 9 October 2024; gazetted 17 October 2024), which amended PDPA governance concepts and introduced new accountability requirements that were commenced in phases beginning in 2025 ("Personal Data Protection (Amendment) Act", 2024).

Several 2024–2025 reforms have direct implications for private-sector biobanking and biobank-adjacent research:

- **Terminology shift to "data controller"**
  Act A1727 substitutes "data controller(s)" for "data user(s)" across the principal Act (with limited exceptions), signalling a closer alignment with international terminology.
- **Expanded "sensitive" category via biometrics**
  "Biometric data" is introduced and explicitly included within "sensitive personal data". This would be relevant where biobanks increasingly use biometric identifiers or biometric-linked systems (e.g., authentication, identity verification).
- **Data processor accountability for security**
  Act A1727 imposes direct compliance responsibility on data processors to comply with the Security Principle, increasing the importance of contractual and technical security controls across vendor chains (e.g., cloud hosting, sequencing service providers, LIMS vendors).
- **Mandatory governance functions**
  A new requirement for appointment of Data Protection Officer(s) by both data controllers and (where processing is carried out on behalf of controllers) data processors.

- **Mandatory breach notification**
  A new requirement for data controllers to notify the regulator "as soon as practicable" upon believing a personal data breach has occurred, and to notify affected data subjects where the breach causes or is likely to cause significant harm.
- **Data portability right**
  A new statutory "right to data portability" allowing data subjects to request transmission of their personal data to another controller (subject to feasibility/compatibility), a provision that may become salient where biobank-linked testing/services are provided in PDPA-covered settings.
- **Cross-border transfer redesign**
  Act A1727 amends Section 129 by deleting the prior "whitelist" prohibition structure (subsection (1)) and reshaping transfer conditions, which may affect governance of international collaborations involving personal data transfers by PDPA-covered entities.

Overall, the PDPA's post-2024 configuration strengthens the compliance expectations for private-sector biobanks and private-sector partners handling health/genomic data, but it does not itself resolve governance issues for public-sector biobanks, given the PDPA's statutory non-application to Federal and State Governments (Abdul Aziz & Mohd Yusof, 2019).

(b) Human Tissues Act 1974 (Act 130)

The Human Tissues Act 1974 is a foundational Malaysian statute addressing tissue use, but its scope is narrower than modern biobanking practice. The Act is framed as legislation concerning the use of parts of human bodies of deceased persons for therapeutic purposes and for purposes of medical education and research ("Human Tissue Act", 1974).

Operationally, it provides a statutory route for post-mortem donation where the deceased expressed wishes, including for research and permits authorisation of removal from the body after death under specified conditions. Because contemporary biobanking often involves living donors, longitudinal collection, large-scale linked datasets, and genomic/omics analysis, it can be argued that the Human Tissues Act 1974 may not fully address contemporary challenges, such as genetic data protection, biobanking, and advanced consent models, even if it remains part of the relevant legal backdrop. This is because the Act is not designed for living-donor research biobanking.

(c) National Guidance on Human Biological Samples and Research Ethics Oversight

A major pillar of Malaysian governance for human sample-based research is the MOH-issued Malaysian Guidelines on the Use of Human Biological Samples for Research (2nd ed., 2025). These guidelines are designed to support ethical and responsible practice across areas such as informed consent, sample governance, confidentiality, data protection, and benefit-sharing (Malaysia Ministry of Health, 2025).

Two statements in the 2025 guidance are particularly important for a legally accurate overview:

- **No single dedicated statute**
  The guidance states that, in Malaysia, there is no single, specific legislation regulating the use of human biological samples in research, and that governance therefore relies on multiple applicable laws and regulatory mechanisms.
- **Transfer governance and custodianship logic**
  The guidance emphasises that inter-institutional and cross-border transfer should be governed by approvals and formal agreements. It explicitly recommends approvals from national and institutional authorities prior to import/export and advises the use of data and material transfer agreements. It further states that stewardship or custodianship (rather than ownership) should be defined via a Material Transfer Agreement (MTA) before transfer, outlining roles/responsibilities of sender and receiver.

The same guidance adopts a strong "sample sovereignty" position, whereby it states that samples from Malaysian participants should not be biobanked or stored outside Malaysia for future research/use, allowing overseas sending only under constrained circumstances (e.g., unavailable technology domestically), requiring case-by-case IRB/IEC review, and prohibiting overseas storage for future use.

It is worth noting that because guidelines are not statutes, their practical force comes through (i) ethics committee requirements, (ii) institutional SOPs and governance policies, and (iii) research contracts and access agreements that operationalise their expectations.

(d) Ministry of Health Research Governance: NMRR and MREC (Public-Sector Pathway)

For studies involving MOH personnel, MOH facilities, MOH patients/data, or MOH funding, Malaysia uses a dedicated administrative pathway via the National Medical Research Register (NMRR) and MOH ethics processes. A MOH NMRR Secretariat training deck describes NMRR as a web-based tool supporting NIH (MOH) guidelines on the conduct of research and enabling online research registration and submission/review/approval workflows.

Crucially for biobank-related research, the same source states that research involving human subjects requires prior review and approval by the Medical Research and Ethics Committee (MREC). This MOH-specific governance pathway is especially important because the PDPA's non-application to Federal/State Government means that public-sector compliance relies heavily on institutional mechanisms (ethics governance, ministerial circulars/guidelines, and internal controls) rather than on the PDPA alone.

(e) Private Healthcare Facilities and Services Act 1998 and Clinical Standards Relevant to Cord Blood Banks

Private-sector biobanking activities that are embedded within private healthcare delivery may be shaped by Malaysia's sectoral regulation of private health services. The Private Healthcare Facilities and Services Act 1998 (Act 586) is an "umbrella" statute providing for regulation and control of private healthcare facilities and services ("Private Healthcare Facilities and Services Act", 1998). Although Act 586 is not a biobank statute, its licensing and regulatory architecture can be relevant where biobanking is operationalised as part of regulated private healthcare services.

For cord blood banking, Malaysia has biobank-adjacent national standards and policy instruments that explicitly include both public and private sectors:

- The MOH National Standards for Cord Blood Banking and Transplantation states its primary objective is to promote quality medical and laboratory practices in both public and private cord blood banks in Malaysia, noting that an earlier edition was published in 2008 (Malaysia Ministry of Health, 2019).
- The MOH National Organ, Tissue and Cell Transplantation Policy (published June 2007) states that the National Cord Blood Banking Programme includes both public and private sectors and "shall be coordinated and regulated" by the MOH; it further states that establishment of public and private cord blood banks shall be in accordance with national standards/guidelines and subject to MOH approval (Malaysia Ministry of Health, 2007).

(f) International Guidelines and Standards Used as Ethical Reference Points

Malaysian research ethics governance frequently draws on well-established international instruments, often via ethics committee practice and national guidance rather than direct statutory incorporation. Three particularly relevant reference "anchors" for biobanking are:

- The World Medical Association's Declaration of Helsinki, which explicitly covers research involving identifiable human material or data and has been revised multiple times (most recently October 2024) (Association, 2024).
- UNESCO's Universal Declaration on Bioethics and Human Rights, a normative instrument anchoring bioethics principles in human dignity, human rights, and fundamental freedoms (UNESCO, 2006).
- The OECD Guidelines on Human Biobanks and Genetic Research Databases (2009), which provide non-binding but influential guidance on

governance, management, access, privacy/confidentiality, and operational policies for biobanks and genetic research databases (OECD, 2009).

These instruments matter analytically because they provide a vocabulary for comparing Malaysian governance, which is largely patchwork and relying on ethics oversight, with jurisdictions that have dedicated statutory regimes for human tissue/biobank governance.

(g) National Bioethics Council of Malaysia (Advisory Role)

Malaysia established the National Bioethics Council of Malaysia (Majlis Bioetika Negara) as an advisory panel to discuss and resolve bioethical issues with broad societal impacts (e.g., environmental, social, health, cultural, legal, and religious dimensions) (Malaysia Ministry of Science, 2012). In the biobanking context, the Council is best understood as part of the wider bioethics governance environment rather than as the primary operational regulator of day-to-day biobank practice, which is more directly shaped by MOH guidance, institutional ethics committees, and applicable statutes.

1.4 Key Challenges in the Regulatory Framework

Although Malaysia has developed substantial ethics guidance and sector-specific standards, several structural challenges remain that are significant for ethical and legal analysis of biobank practice.

1.4.1 Absence of a Dedicated National "Biobank Act" and Reliance on Patchwork Governance

Malaysia has repeatedly been described, both in national guidance and scholarly discussion, as lacking a single, specific legislation governing biobanking. This produces a governance structure that relies on general statutes (data protection, healthcare regulation, post-mortem tissue use), ethics committee oversight, and institutional governance documents (Abdul Aziz & Mohd Yusof, 2019; Bin Abdul Aziz, 2018; Rahman, 2025).

A practical implication is that key issues, such as secondary use governance, re-consent thresholds, governance of withdrawal, and governance of long-term custodianship across institutions, may be addressed unevenly depending on the biobank's host institution and sector (Amin et al., 2021).

1.4.2 Divergent Public-Sector and Private-Sector Compliance Pathways (Data Protection Boundary Problem)

A core legal complexity is that the PDPA regulates personal data in commercial transactions and does not apply to Federal and State Governments, while many significant health research infrastructures are government-linked.

This creates a regulatory asymmetry, whereby private-sector biobanks face strengthened PDPA accountability (including DPO appointment and breach notification requirements), whereas public-sector biobanks rely on administrative governance (e.g., MOH guidance, ethics review mechanisms, institutional rules).

From an ethical lens, this could also complicate public messaging and trust building, because "privacy protections" may appear different across sectors even where sensitive data types and risks are similar.

1.4.3 Consent for Long-Term Storage and Secondary Use (Breadth, Legitimacy, and Public Understanding)

Biobanking raises persistent questions about what consent model is ethically and legally sufficient for future unspecified research. Malaysian scholarship notes that empirical work on informed consent in Malaysian biobanking has historically been limited and that questions about governance, public awareness, and legitimacy remain pressing (Abdul Aziz & Mohd Yusof, 2019; Amin et al., 2021).

This is particularly salient in multi-ethnic settings and in biobanks linked to clinical care, where the risk of therapeutic misconception and misunderstandings about future data use may be higher unless consent processes are carefully designed and sustained.

1.4.4 Cross-Border Data and Sample Sharing (Loss of Control, Sovereignty, and Harmonisation Pressures)

Modern biomedical research depends on collaboration and, often, cross-border transfer of data and samples. Yet, cross-border sharing heightens concerns about loss of control, downstream use, and accountability. MOH guidance adopts a restrictive stance, stating that Malaysian participant samples should not be biobanked/stored overseas for future use, and that overseas sending should be limited and strictly governed (including IRB/IEC review and prohibition of overseas storage for future use) (Malaysia Ministry of Health, 2025).

In parallel, the PDPA's amended cross-border transfer rules, where PDPA applies, require organisations to align transfers with the post-2024 statutory conditions, now framed differently after the amendment ("Personal Data Protection (Amendment) Act", 2024). These dual regimes can create operational friction for collaborations spanning public and private partners, and they further underscore the importance of formal MTAs/DTAs and transparent governance documentation.

1.4.5 Commercialisation, Benefit-Sharing, and Perceived Legitimacy

Commercial involvement can be ethically contentious in biobanking because it raises questions about benefit-sharing, exploitation, and erosion of trust.

A MOH technical report on biorepositories notes that commercialisation of biobank samples is not categorically prohibited under relevant guidance, but it is contingent on donors being informed and consenting to such activity (as interpreted in that report) (Working Committee for the Establishment of the National Biorepository Policy for Malaysia, 2023).

For private/clinical-adjacent biobanking activities, especially cord blood banks, Malaysia's policy landscape indicates that both public and private sectors operate under national standards and MOH approval expectations, reflecting an attempt to manage legitimacy through quality/safety governance (Malaysia Ministry of Health, 2007). Nevertheless, it can be argued that public trust can decrease when commercial actors are involved, underscoring the need for robust transparency, conflict-of-interest management, and credible governance commitments (Bin Abdul Aziz, 2018).

1.4.6 Standardisation and Capacity for Sustained Governance (Quality Systems, Funding, and Oversight Coordination)

Malaysia's policy and technical documents reflect active efforts to improve biorepository infrastructure and to articulate a national policy direction (e.g., concept notes for national biorepositories) (Working Committee for the Establishment of the National Biorepository Policy for Malaysia, 2023). However, sustained governance requires resources, such as standard operating procedures, trained personnel, auditability, secure IT systems, and long-term funding models. MOH guidance emphasises the importance of sample integrity, tracking systems, and regulatory compliance across the sample lifecycle (Malaysia Ministry of Health, 2025).

The practical challenge is that Malaysia's biobank ecosystem spans multiple host institutions and sectors, so achieving consistent operational standards and interoperable governance mechanisms (including harmonised review practices across IRBs/IECs) remains a continuing governance question rather than a solved problem (Amin et al., 2021).

1.4.7 Identifiability and Re-Identification Risk in Genomic and Linked Datasets

Even where samples/data are coded, genomic data and richly linked metadata increase re-identification risks, complicating promises of anonymity and raising questions about proportionate security, controlled access, and governance of data linkage.

1.5 Conclusion

Malaysia's biobanking governance landscape is best understood as a composite regime, which involves general statutes (data protection, private healthcare regulation, and post-mortem tissue governance) that operate alongside national guidance, institutional ethics oversight, and contractual governance (MTAs/DTAs) to manage access, sharing, confidentiality, and accountability.

From an up-to-date legal perspective, two conclusions are especially important for this book's framing. First, Malaysia still lacks a single, biobank-specific statute, which means ethical legitimacy and legal compliance depend heavily on the strength and consistency of ethics review, institutional governance, transparency practices, and enforceable agreements. Second, the PDPA's 2024 amendments (in force in phases through 2025) materially strengthen private-sector data governance through new accountability (DPO), breach notification, and security responsibilities that are highly relevant for commercial/private biobank contexts, even as the public-sector pathway remains shaped by ministry governance systems and ethics mechanisms.

These features make Malaysia a particularly instructive setting for the hypothetical case studies developed in this book – the ethical dilemmas of consent, privacy, commercialisation, incidental findings, and cross-border sharing arise not in a vacuum, but within a governance environment where ethical oversight and institutional stewardship often do as much practical work as statute. Accordingly, the case studies in subsequent chapters are structured to test governance "stress points" where statutory coverage is partial, guidance is normatively demanding but non-binding, and institutional practices vary across sectors.

References

Abdul Aziz, M. F., & Mohd Yusof, A. N. (2019). Can dynamic consent facilitate the protection of biomedical big data in biobanking in Malaysia? *Asian Bioethics Review*, *11*(2), 209–222. https://pmc.ncbi.nlm.nih.gov/articles/PMC7747242/

Amin, L., Olesen, A., Mahadi, Z., & Ibrahim, M. (2021). Current status and future challenges of biobank research in Malaysia. *Asian Bioethics Review*, *13*(3), 297–315. https://doi.org/10.1007/s41649-021-00171-5

Bin Abdul Aziz, M. F. (2018). *Malaysian biobanks: Is the current governance framework adequate?* (p. 1). https://law.um.edu.my/menu%20-%20research%20files/CELEST%20files/CELEST%20NEWSLETTER/CELEST%20%282018%29%20Issue%201%20Malaysian%20biobanks.%20is%20the%20current%20governance%20framework%20adequate.pdf

CryoCord Sdn Bhd. Retrieved January 12, 2026, from https://cryocord.com.my/?gad_source=1

Human Tissue Act. (1974).

Jamal, R., Syed Zakaria, S. Z., Kamaruddin, M. A., Abd Jalal, N., Ismail, N., Mohd Kamil, N., Abdullah, N., Baharudin, N., Hussin, N. H., Othman, H., & Mahadi, N. M. (2015). Cohort profile: The Malaysian cohort (TMC) project: A prospective study of non-communicable diseases in a multi-ethnic population. *The International Journal of Epidemiology*, *44*(2), 423–431. https://doi.org/10.1093/ije/dyu089

Malaysia Ministry of Science, Technology and Innovation. (2012). *Pelancaran Majlis Bioetika Negara*. Retrieved December 12, 2025, from https://www.mosti.gov.my/en/berita/pelancaran-majlis-bioetika-negara/

The Working Committee for the Establishment of the National Biorepository Policy for Malaysia. (2023). A Tecnical Report: The Roadmap to Establishing the National Biorepository Policy for Malaysia. National Laboratory Technical Advisory Committee (LTAC). Retrieved January 12, 2026, from https://mkak.moh.gov.my/index.php/muat-turun/penerbitan?download=33:technical-report-concept-note-biorepositories-p-g-edited-22-aug-2023

The Malaysian Cohort. Universiti Kebangsaan Malaysia. Retrieved December 25, 2025, from https://www.ukm.my/mycohort/ms/

Malaysian Guidelines on the Use of Human Biological Samples for Research. (2025). Malaysia Ministry of Health.

National Organ, Tissue and Cell Transplantation Policy. (2007). Malaysia Ministry of Health.

National Standards for Cord Blood Banking and Transplantation. (2019). Malaysia Ministry of Health.

OECD Guidelines and Human Biobanks and Genetic Research Databases. (2009) OECD.

Personal Data Protection Act. (2010).

Personal Data Protection (Amendment) Act. (2024).

Private Healthcare Facilities and Services Act. (1998).

Rahman, S. (2025). Expert opinion bioethics and biobanking in biomedical research in Malaysia. *IIUM Medical Journal Malaysia*, *24*, 4–7. https://doi.org/10.31436/imjm.v24i03.2903

StemLife Berhad. Retrieved January 12, 2026, from https://www.stemlife.com/en

Universal Declaration on Bioethics and Human Rights. (2006). UNESCO.

Vaithilingam, R. D., Safii, S. H., Baharuddin, N. A., Karen-Ng, L. P., Saub, R., Ariffin, F., Ramli, H., Sharifuddin, A., Hidayat, M. F., Raman, R., Chan, Y. K., Rani, N. A., Rahim, R. A., Shahruddin, N., Cheong, S. C., Bartold, P. M., & Zain, R. B. (2015). Establishing and managing a periodontal biobank for research: The sharing of experience. *Oral Diseases*, *21*(1), e62–e69. https://doi.org/10.1111/odi.12267

WMA Declaration of Helsinki – Ethical Principles for Medical Research Involving Human Participants. (2024). Association.

Zain, R. B., Athirajan, V., Ghani, W. M., Razak, I. A., Raja Latifah, R. J., Ismail, S. M., Sallam, A. A., Bustam, A. Z., Rahman, Z. A., Hussien, A., Talib, N., Cheong, S. C., & Jallaludin, A. (2013). An oral cancer biobank initiative: A platform for multidisciplinary research in a developing country. *Cell Tissue Bank*, *14*(1), 45–52. https://doi.org/10.1007/s10561-012-9298-0

2 Informed Consent in Biobanking

2.1 The Concept of Informed Consent

Informed consent is a fundamental principle of ethical medical and scientific research, ensuring that individuals are made adequately aware of the implications of participation and voluntarily agree to the collection and use of their biological materials and associated data. Within the context of biobanking, however, informed consent assumes a distinct complexity. Unlike conventional clinical research, where objectives, duration, and procedures are typically defined at enrolment, biobanking involves long-term storage of biospecimens and the possibility of future research uses that may not yet be conceived at the time of donation. Consent, therefore, becomes less a single authorisation and more an **ongoing governance relationship** between participants and research institutions.

Scholarly discourse increasingly recognises that the traditional model of study-specific consent is often impractical for biobanking, particularly in large population-based or longitudinal repositories. As a result, alternative consent models have emerged, including **broad consent, tiered consent, and dynamic consent**, each attempting to balance participant autonomy with research feasibility (Abdul Aziz & Mohd Yusof, 2019). Broad consent permits the future use of samples within ethically defined parameters, whereas dynamic consent introduces interactive digital platforms that allow participants to modify their preferences over time. Empirical reviews suggest that dynamic consent can enhance participant engagement, communication, and trust, although challenges such as digital exclusion and consent fatigue remain significant considerations (Lay et al., 2025).

The evolution of consent practices is also closely tied to questions of inclusivity and representation. Contemporary analyses emphasise that consent is not merely an informational exercise but a mechanism for addressing historical mistrust and ensuring ethical engagement with under-represented or marginalised communities. Ethical biobanking therefore requires culturally sensitive communication, transparency in governance, and recognition of the social contexts in which consent is sought (Lee et al., 2025). In this sense, informed consent functions not only as an individual safeguard but also as a collective trust-building tool within diverse research ecosystems.

DOI: 10.4324/9781003745785-2

In addition to procedural models, recent theoretical work has questioned whether ethically valid consent must always be grounded in detailed cognitive understanding. Some scholars propose that, in low-risk and well-governed biobank environments, **justified trust in a trustworthy institution** may ethically complement or partially substitute for exhaustive informational comprehension, provided voluntariness and institutional accountability are preserved (Byrnes, 2025). This perspective reframes consent as a relational and institutional phenomenon rather than a purely transactional disclosure process.

Within Southeast Asian and hospital-based biobank contexts, practical experiences further demonstrate that consent design must accommodate operational realities, literacy levels, and institutional workflows. Studies of academic hospital biobanks show that carefully structured broad consent models, combined with ethics committee oversight and clear governance documentation, can achieve both ethical sufficiency and practical feasibility when tailored to local contexts (Hartanti et al., 2025).

In operational terms, informed consent in biobanking typically requires disclosure of several interrelated elements:

2.1.1 What Is Being Collected?

The types of biological samples, such as blood, saliva, tissue, or genomic data, and any associated personal or clinical information.

2.1.2 How Will the Samples Be Used?

Whether use is confined to a specific project or extends to future, unspecified, or secondary research.

2.1.3 Who Will Have Access to the Samples and Data?

Including domestic or international collaborations, data-sharing arrangements, and potential commercial partnerships.

2.1.4 Risks and Potential Benefits Involved

Such as privacy breaches, re-identification risks, or broader societal and scientific benefits.

2.1.5 Withdrawal Rights and Limitations

Participants should be informed of their right to withdraw consent and the practical implications of withdrawal, particularly where anonymised data or completed analyses are concerned.

2.1.6 Communication of Incidental Findings and Updates

Where relevant, participants should be informed whether clinically significant incidental findings or research updates will be returned.

These informational components are increasingly complemented by broader ethical considerations, transparency of governance, data security, community engagement, and institutional trustworthiness, reflecting the contemporary understanding that consent in biobanking is **dynamic, relational, and embedded within a wider framework of ethical stewardship rather than a singular signed document.**

2.2 Ethical Importance of Informed Consent in Biobanking

The ethical importance of informed consent in biobanking extends beyond procedural compliance and is closely intertwined with broader principles of autonomy, trust, justice, and social responsibility. Biobanks store biological materials and data that may retain scientific and informational value long after initial collection, often across multiple research projects and jurisdictions. As such, consent mechanisms operate not merely as administrative requirements but as ethical safeguards that mediate the relationship between individuals and research institutions over time.

2.2.1 Respect for Autonomy

Respect for autonomy remains the most immediate ethical justification for informed consent. Individuals retain moral authority over decisions relating to their bodies, genetic information, and personal data. In the biobanking context, this principle is complicated by the uncertainty of future research uses and the possibility that participants may not foresee all potential implications at the time of donation. Contemporary scholarship emphasises that autonomy in biobanking should therefore be understood as ongoing and revisable, rather than static, reinforcing the need for mechanisms such as re-consent options or dynamic consent platforms that allow participants to revisit their decisions over time (Lay et al., 2025).

2.2.2 Transparency and Institutional Trust

Biobanks rely fundamentally on voluntary participation and sustained public confidence. Transparency regarding governance structures, data-sharing arrangements, and oversight mechanisms fosters trust and mitigates perceptions of exploitation or misuse. Ethical analyses increasingly highlight that trust is not merely interpersonal but **institutional**, grounded in demonstrable accountability, regulatory compliance, and effective communication. Where transparency is weak or inconsistent, public willingness to contribute biological materials may decline, undermining both the legitimacy and sustainability of research infrastructures (Lee et al., 2025).

2.2.3 Protection of Participants' Rights and Privacy

Informed consent also functions as a protective mechanism for participants' rights to privacy, confidentiality, and informational control. Biological samples, particularly those linked to genomic or longitudinal data, carry risks of re-identification and misuse if safeguards are inadequate. Ethical biobanking therefore requires not only disclosure of risks but also the implementation of data security measures, restricted access protocols, and clear withdrawal procedures. The recognition that consent cannot be fully meaningful without parallel governance protections has led scholars to emphasise consent-plus-governance models, where ethical legitimacy derives from both participant authorisation and institutional safeguards (Byrnes, 2025).

2.2.4 Minimisation of Harm

Biobank research may expose participants to non-physical harms, including psychological distress, discrimination, or social stigmatisation arising from genetic or health-related findings. The consent process provides an opportunity to communicate these risks, manage expectations, and clarify the handling of incidental findings or return-of-results policies. Empirical work in hospital-based and population biobanks shows that participants value clarity regarding these issues, suggesting that well-designed consent processes can reduce uncertainty and enhance perceived fairness (Hartanti et al., 2025).

2.2.5 Equity, Inclusion, and Justice

Beyond individual rights, informed consent carries a distributive and social justice dimension. Historically under-represented communities may face linguistic, cultural, or socio-economic barriers that impede meaningful participation in research. Ethical consent practices must therefore be inclusive, culturally sensitive, and accessible, ensuring that participation is neither coerced nor structurally exclusionary. Recent scholarship underscores that inclusive consent practices contribute not only to fairness but also to scientific validity by promoting representative datasets and reducing health disparities (Lee et al., 2025).

2.2.6 Trust, Understanding, and Ethical Sufficiency

Emerging theoretical discussions have further questioned whether ethically valid consent must always be grounded in comprehensive cognitive understanding. As highlighted earlier, in low-risk and well-governed biobank environments, some scholars argue that justified trust in trustworthy institutions may ethically complement or partially substitute for detailed informational comprehension, provided voluntariness and institutional accountability are maintained (Byrnes, 2025). This perspective does not negate the importance of disclosure but recognises that ethical legitimacy may also rest on the quality of governance and institutional integrity, not solely on the quantity of information conveyed.

Overall, these considerations demonstrate that informed consent in biobanking operates at the intersection of personal autonomy, institutional ethics, and social justice. It is both a protective device for individual participants and a legitimising mechanism for research systems, reinforcing the notion that ethical biobanking depends as much on trustworthy governance and inclusive engagement as it does on the formal act of signing a consent document.

2.3 Regulatory Framework for Informed Consent in Malaysia

As shown in the preceding chapter, Malaysia does not currently have a single comprehensive statute dedicated exclusively to biobanking. Therefore, informed consent obligations arise from a multi-layered combination of statutory law, national ethical guidelines, institutional review mechanisms, and international soft-law standards. This layered structure means that compliance is not confined to one legal source but depends on the interaction between data protection law, professional duties, and sector-specific ethical instruments.

2.3.1 Malaysian Guidelines on the Use of Human Biological Samples for Research (2nd ed., 2025)

The Malaysian Guidelines on the Use of Human Biological Samples for Research is the most directly relevant national instrument governing the ethical collection, storage, transfer, and use of biological materials. Although not enacted as legislation, it functions as a quasi-regulatory national standard widely relied upon by universities, hospitals, and research institutions.

Key consent-related elements include:

- Recognition of specific, broad, and electronic consent models
- Requirement for Institutional Review Board (IRB) / Ethics Committee approval
- Explicit articulation of withdrawal and re-consent mechanisms
- Emphasis on language accessibility and cultural sensitivity
- Disclosure obligations relating to commercial involvement and international data transfer
- Guidance on posthumous use of samples
- Introduction of custodianship rather than ownership, positioning institutions as stewards rather than proprietors of biological materials

The Guideline also integrates references to other Malaysian statutes, such as the Human Tissues Act and the Personal Data Protection Act, thereby serving as a practical bridge between ethical expectations and legal compliance.

2.3.2 Personal Data Protection Act 2010 (PDPA) and 2024 Amendments

The **PDPA** forms the primary statutory backbone for consent relating to personal and sensitive personal data, including health and genetic information. Although it is not biobank-specific, its provisions are directly applicable to the handling of identifiable biological data.

Core consent-relevant principles include:

- Explicit consent requirement for sensitive personal data
- Purpose limitation, restricting use to disclosed objectives
- Notice and Choice obligations, requiring participants to be informed of data usage and disclosure
- Security safeguards against unauthorised access or misuse
- Rights of access, correction, and withdrawal of consent

The 2024 amendments strengthen accountability expectations and modernise terminology, reinforcing the obligation of institutions to maintain transparent and responsible data governance practices.

2.3.3 Institutional Review Boards (IRBs) and Research Ethics Committees

Ethics review bodies function as the **primary enforcement mechanism** for consent standards in practice. All research involving human biological materials is expected to undergo review before commencement.

Their roles include:

- Assessing clarity and proportionality of consent forms
- Evaluating risk–benefit balance
- Ensuring protection of vulnerable populations
- Monitoring ongoing compliance and amendments

In many respects, IRBs act as the practical interface between abstract ethical principles and day-to-day research conduct.

2.3.4 Professional and Clinical Governance Instruments

Additional guidance arises from professional and clinical standards, including:

- **Malaysian Guideline for Good Clinical Practice (GCP)** – requiring written informed consent, investigator accountability, and ethics review.

- **Malaysian Code of Responsible Conduct in Research** – emphasising integrity, transparency, and responsible data stewardship.
- **Malaysian Medical Council Guidelines** – reinforcing duties of confidentiality, autonomy, and professional responsibility, particularly for registered medical practitioners.

These instruments collectively reinforce that consent is not solely a research obligation but also a professional ethical duty.

2.3.5 International Ethical Frameworks

Malaysian biobank practices are also interpretively influenced by global ethical instruments that provide normative guidance where domestic law is silent or general in nature. Commonly referenced frameworks include:

- Declaration of Helsinki – voluntary and adequately informed participation
- CIOMS International Ethical Guidelines – comprehension, vulnerability protection, and secondary data use
- OECD Guidelines on Human Biobanks and Genetic Research Databases – governance, custodianship, and transparency
- UNESCO Universal Declaration on Bioethics and Human Rights – dignity, autonomy, justice, and solidarity

These international standards do not override Malaysian law but shape ethical interpretation and institutional best practices, particularly in cross-border or collaborative research.

Informed consent in Malaysian biobanking is therefore best understood as operating within a layered governance ecosystem rather than a single regulatory regime. Statutory data protection law provides enforceable legal duties; national guidelines translate ethical principles into operational expectations; IRBs ensure institutional accountability; and international frameworks supply interpretive depth. Together, these layers form a complementary structure that seeks to balance participant autonomy, data protection, and scientific advancement while maintaining public trust in biomedical research.

2.4 Case Studies

2.4.1 Case Study 1: The Ambiguous Consent

Case Narrative

Mr. Raj is a 45-year-old factory worker living in a rural area of Malaysia. He has a family history of diabetes and hypertension and, after a recent health screening, is advised by his physician to participate in a university hospital study examining genetic markers for chronic diseases. The hospital is developing a national biobank for non-communicable diseases.

At his appointment, Mr. Raj is given a consent form explaining the collection of blood and urine samples together with his medical history. The form briefly states that the research concerns "genetic and environmental risk factors for chronic diseases" and contains a sentence indicating that "genetic information derived from collected samples can be used for subsequent research." The language is technical, and the staff member provides minimal explanation, stating only that signing is necessary if he agrees to participate.

Mr. Raj signs, assuming this is a routine medical procedure. He is unaware that his samples may later be used in unrelated studies, shared internationally, or involved in commercial pharmaceutical research.

Several years later, Mr. Raj is informed that his DNA contributed to a pharmaceutical company's diabetes drug research and may also be shared with international research networks. He feels misled and distressed, believing he was not adequately informed about the scope of future use or commercial involvement.

The situation raises fundamental ethical concerns about whether the consent obtained was genuinely informed or merely procedural, and whether institutional transparency and participant autonomy were sufficiently respected.

Commentary

(A) THE COMPLEXITY OF INFORMED CONSENT IN BIOBANKING

Mr. Raj's situation illustrates a recurring ethical issue in biobank governance involving ambiguous or over-generalised consent. Biobanks often operate on long temporal horizons where future research uses are uncertain, leading institutions to rely on broad or blanket consent formulations. Broad consent is widely accepted as ethically permissible under certain conditions, but it can be argued that its validity depends on clarity of boundaries, transparency of governance, and effective communication rather than the mere presence of a signature.

As highlighted earlier, an empirical and comparative study of hospital-based biobanks in Southeast Asia similarly demonstrate that broad consent can be ethically sufficient only when accompanied by strong ethics committee oversight, clear disclosure of commercial and international data-sharing possibilities, and accessible language (Hartanti et al., 2025). Where such safeguards are absent, consent risks becoming symbolic rather than substantive.

Dynamic consent models have been proposed as one response to this challenge, allowing participants to revisit and modify their preferences over time through digital platforms. Systematic reviews indicate that dynamic consent can enhance engagement and trust, although it may also introduce concerns such as digital exclusion and consent fatigue (Lay et al., 2025). In the Malaysian context, it has been argued that dynamic or interactive consent mechanisms may better align with the principles embedded in the Personal Data Protection Act 2010 by reinforcing autonomy and data integrity (Abdul Aziz & Mohd Yusof, 2019).

(B) CHALLENGES IN UNDERSTANDING CONSENT FORMS

A central issue in this case is comprehension. Consent forms are frequently drafted in legal or technical terminology that is inaccessible to individuals without specialised knowledge. In multicultural and multilingual societies such as Malaysia, disparities in literacy, language proficiency, and educational background may further complicate understanding.

Research across diverse jurisdictions has consistently shown that participants often sign consent forms without full comprehension, particularly when documents are lengthy or overly technical (Hartanti et al., 2025). This phenomenon does not necessarily indicate negligence on the part of participants; rather, it highlights structural communication barriers and institutional responsibility to ensure clarity. Ethical consent therefore requires not only disclosure but also effective communication and verification of understanding.

(C) ETHICAL IMPLICATIONS: AUTONOMY, TRUST, AND FAIRNESS

The ethical concerns in Mr. Raj's case revolve around three interrelated principles:

Autonomy Autonomy is compromised when individuals are unaware of material facts that could influence their decision. The absence of disclosure regarding commercial partnerships or international data transfer limits meaningful choice.

Trust Biobanking depends on sustained public trust. Studies on under-represented communities emphasise that transparency, cultural sensitivity, and continuous engagement are essential to maintaining this trust. When participants perceive that information has been withheld, institutional credibility suffers.

Fairness and Justice Fairness requires equitable treatment and transparent communication of both risks and potential benefits. Where biological materials contribute to commercial innovation, questions arise concerning recognition, benefit sharing, or at minimum informed acknowledgement. International bioethics discourse increasingly frames consent as part of a broader justice-oriented governance framework, rather than as an isolated procedural step.

(D) REGULATORY REQUIREMENTS FOR INFORMED CONSENT IN MALAYSIA

Malaysia's consent obligations for biobanking arise from a layered regulatory ecosystem combining statutory law, national guidelines, and institutional ethics oversight.

Personal Data Protection Act 2010 (PDPA) The PDPA establishes legally enforceable duties of explicit consent, purpose limitation, disclosure control, data security, and withdrawal rights. Genetic and health data fall within "sensitive personal data", requiring heightened safeguards. In Mr. Raj's case, failure to adequately inform him of international data transfer or secondary commercial use may conflict with the PDPA's Notice and Choice and Disclosure Principles.

Malaysian Guidelines on the Use of Human Biological Samples for Research (2nd ed., 2025) This sector-specific guideline explicitly recognises broad and digital consent but requires:

- clarity of future research scope,
- explanation of data sharing and commercialisation possibilities,
- withdrawal and re-consent mechanisms, and
- language accessibility and cultural sensitivity.

Institutional Review Boards (IRBs) / Ethics Committees All human biological sample research must undergo ethics review. IRBs are responsible for ensuring that consent forms are clear, proportionate, and reflective of current ethical standards.

(E) INTERNATIONAL ETHICAL STANDARDS

Malaysia's regulatory approach is further informed by international instruments such as:

- **Declaration of Helsinki** – requiring voluntary and adequately informed consent.
- **CIOMS International Ethical Guidelines** – emphasising comprehension, vulnerability protection, and future data use disclosure.
- **OECD Guidelines on Human Biobanks** – addressing governance, custodianship, and transparency.
- **UNESCO Universal Declaration on Bioethics and Human Rights** – highlighting autonomy, dignity, and justice.

These frameworks collectively reinforce that consent in biobanking must be transparent, revisable, and supported by institutional accountability, not merely documented.

(F) ENSURING COMPREHENSIVENESS IN INFORMED CONSENT

Mr. Raj's case underscores the importance of designing consent processes that are both ethically robust and practically accessible:

1. Plain-language, multilingual consent forms
2. Interactive verbal explanations and question-and-answer sessions

3. Periodic re-consent or dynamic consent mechanisms
4. Visual and multimedia aids
5. Continuous IRB and governance oversight

Empirical evidence indicates that digital and interactive consent tools can significantly improve participant understanding and engagement when complemented by non-digital alternatives to avoid exclusion.

Key Takeaways

- **Clarity of future use is central to ethical consent.**
  Participants must understand that biobank participation may extend beyond the immediate study into secondary, commercial, or international research. Vague wording undermines autonomy, even if a signature is obtained.
- **Comprehension is the true benchmark of validity.**
  Ethical consent is measured by what participants actually understand, not by the completeness of documentation. Plain language and interactive explanation are therefore integral, not optional.
- **Broad consent is defensible only with strong safeguards.**
  Oversight by ethics committees, clear withdrawal mechanisms, and transparent governance structures are what transform broad consent from a convenience into an ethically legitimate model.

2.4.2 Case Study 2: Culturally Discordant Consent in a Rural Malay-Muslim Context

Case Narrative

Mrs. Aisyah is a 60-year-old Malay Muslim woman living in a semi-urban area in Kelantan. As a regular patient at a government clinic, she is invited to participate in a community-based genetic research study aimed at identifying cancer risk factors among the Malay population. The project is led by a local university in collaboration with an international research institute and involves establishing a biobank for future, unspecified research.

During a clinic visit, a nurse provides Mrs. Aisyah with an information leaflet and consent form written in Bahasa Malaysia. The form seeks her agreement to donate blood and cheek-swab samples that may be stored and used for future genetic studies. It also indicates that samples may be shared with international collaborators, including private pharmaceutical companies.

Although Mrs. Aisyah is literate in Bahasa Malaysia, she struggles to understand technical terms such as *genomic sequencing*, *international data sharing*, and *future unspecified research*. She is particularly concerned about the use of her samples after death and whether such use aligns with her religious beliefs. However, out of respect for healthcare authority figures and cultural norms of politeness and deference – a common sentiment shared among the local community – she feels uncomfortable voicing these concerns. She signs the form, assuming it is part of routine medical procedure and trusting that the clinic will act in her best interest.

Two years later, Mrs. Aisyah reads a news article stating that the research project has partnered with a European pharmaceutical company and that Malaysian genetic samples have been transferred abroad for commercial research. She becomes distressed, realising she did not fully appreciate the implications of international and commercial use. She is also troubled by the possibility that her biological materials may continue to be used posthumously in ways that conflict with her religious understanding of bodily sanctity.

Commentary

The case of Mrs. Aisyah illustrates how informed consent in Malaysia cannot be understood purely through legal or procedural lenses. Instead, it reveals the interaction between religious belief, cultural norms, literacy, and institutional communication, particularly among older participants in rural or semi-urban communities.

(A) RELIGIOUS CONCERNS ABOUT BODILY INTEGRITY AND POSTHUMOUS USE

Within Islamic ethical thought, the human body is often understood as an *amanah* (a trust) that must be treated with dignity both in life and after death. Although Islamic jurisprudence is not monolithic, and many scholars support biomedical research for public benefit, uncertainty surrounding posthumous use of tissues may generate discomfort when consent forms do not explicitly address these issues. The absence of clear options to limit or condition post-mortem use can therefore undermine both religious reassurance and perceived moral agency.

From an ethical governance perspective, this concern aligns with broader international principles of respect for dignity and autonomy reflected in global bioethics instruments, which emphasise the right of participants to determine the extent and duration of sample use (UNESCO, 2006).

(B) COMMERCIAL USE AND PERCEIVED EXPLOITATION

Mrs. Aisyah's distress is also linked to the discovery that her samples contributed to pharmaceutical research. Although commercial collaboration is not inherently unethical, lack of explicit disclosure may create a perception of exploitation or unfairness. Scholarly work highlights that transparency regarding commercial partnerships, particularly involving under-represented populations, is critical for maintaining trust and preventing feelings of misuse or commodification of bodily materials (Lee et al., 2025; Tone-Pah-Hote & Redvers, 2022).

Malaysian regulatory instruments similarly stress that consent documentation should clearly state potential commercial involvement and secondary data uses, reinforcing that ethical legitimacy depends on openness rather than the absence of profit.

(C) INTERNATIONAL DATA TRANSFER AND MORAL UNCERTAINTY

Cross-border data sharing introduces additional layers of uncertainty, particularly for participants who fear loss of oversight once samples leave national jurisdiction. These concerns are not unique to religious communities; they are widely recognised in global bioethics discourse as issues of data sovereignty and governance accountability. International guidelines on biobanking emphasise that participants must be informed when samples may be transferred abroad and reassured that equivalent ethical safeguards apply (OECD, 2009).

In the Malaysian context, this obligation is reinforced by national guidelines governing the use of human biological samples, which explicitly require disclosure of international collaborations and data transfer arrangements.

(D) UNDERSTANDING AS A PRECONDITION FOR VALID CONSENT

A central ethical issue in this case is comprehension. Even though the form was in Bahasa Malaysia, linguistic accessibility did not guarantee conceptual understanding. It can be argued that participants, particularly older adults or those unfamiliar with biomedical language, may sign forms without fully grasping technical terminology.

(E) CULTURAL DEFERENCE AND POWER DYNAMICS

Malay cultural norms often emphasise politeness (*budi bahasa*) and respect for authority (*hormat*), especially toward healthcare professionals. These values foster social harmony, but they may also discourage questioning or refusal, resulting in passive compliance rather than active consent. Ethical consent processes must therefore account for power asymmetries and communication barriers, not merely linguistic translation.

(F) RELIGIOUS AND CULTURAL CONCERNS IN BIOBANK CONSENT

To ensure that informed consent is culturally and religiously responsive while remaining ethically robust, several practical strategies may be adopted:

1. Contextualised Consent Options This approach will allow participants to set conditions regarding posthumous use, commercial partnerships, or international transfer.

2. Engagement with Religious and Community Advisors Consultation with recognised bioethics or religious advisory bodies can provide reassurance and contextual legitimacy.

3. Plain-Language and Dialect-Sensitive Materials It is imperative to employ simplified terminology supported by oral explanations and visual aids.

4. Culturally Sensitive Communication Training Communication training is particularly relevant in culturally sensitive settings, whereby research staff need to be able to encourage participants to ask questions without embarrassment or perceived disrespect.

5. Religious and Ethical FAQs Researchers could include brief explanatory sections in a participant information sheet addressing common moral concerns, especially related to religious issues.

Key Takeaways

- **Consent must resonate with religious and moral frameworks.**
  Participants may evaluate biomedical participation through spiritual or ethical lenses. Ignoring these dimensions risks moral discomfort, even where legal requirements are met.
- **Cultural norms can silence genuine hesitation.**
  Deference to healthcare authority and politeness may lead to passive compliance rather than active agreement. Ethical practice requires inviting questions and reducing perceived hierarchy.
- **Transparency about the research plan, including commercialisation and foreign use, prevents moral distress.**
  Participants are less troubled by a research plan, especially commercialisation and international collaboration, when it is disclosed early and framed clearly; distress usually arises from discovery rather than from the activity itself.

2.4.3 Case Study 3: Community Consent and the Ethics of Inclusion – The Orang Asli Context

Case Narrative

In a collaborative research project between a Malaysian university and an international genomics institute, researchers set out to study genetic adaptations to environmental stressors in Indigenous populations. A team of scientists visits a remote Temiar Orang Asli village in Perak to collect saliva and blood samples. The stated objective is to understand population-level genetic diversity in Malaysia and to identify potential protective genes against infectious diseases.

Researchers first meet the village head (*tok batin*) and obtain his verbal approval to begin recruitment. Individual community members are then approached and given consent forms written in Bahasa Malaysia explaining that samples will be stored in a long-term biobank and used for future, unspecified research, including international collaborations. Some individuals sign, influenced by trust in the village leader and attracted by the offer of basic health screenings as part of the engagement.

Weeks later, a regional Indigenous rights non-governmental organisation (NGO) raises concerns. It argues that the consent process did not align with Temiar customary decision-making structures, which typically require broader consultation among elders and kin groups for matters affecting the community collectively. Additional issues are raised regarding language comprehension, lack of community-level benefit sharing, and insufficient disclosure of long-term data usage. There is also concern that the community was not informed that their genetic materials might be analysed alongside other ethnic groups, potentially affecting cultural identity and public perception.

The university responds that individual written consent was obtained and ethical clearance granted by an Institutional Review Board (IRB). Nevertheless, the incident triggers public debate about whether conventional individual-autonomy consent models adequately address Indigenous worldviews, where collective identity and relational decision-making are central.

Commentary

This case illustrates a recurring ethical tension in research governance – namely, the interaction between **individual consent and collective community authority**. Although modern research ethics frameworks emphasise individual autonomy, many Indigenous societies, including Malaysia's Orang Asli communities, embed decision-making within communal structures and intergenerational relationships.

(A) COMMUNITY AS THE ETHICAL UNIT

For many Indigenous groups, ethical agency is not solely individual but rather relational and collective. Decisions concerning access to biological materials or cultural knowledge may be understood as affecting the community as a whole. International bioethics scholarship increasingly recognises that applying purely individualistic consent frameworks in such settings risks ethical misalignment and perceived disrespect (Fitzpatrick et al., 2016; Garrison et al., 2020, 2019; Tsosie et al., 2019)

Securing verbal approval from a *tok batin* may represent a culturally respectful first step, but it does not necessarily substitute for broader consultation. Authority within Orang Asli communities is often distributed rather than hierarchical, and research affecting shared identity or heritage may require deliberation among elders and kin networks.

This tension is further reflected at the regulatory level. The Malaysian Guidelines on the Use of Human Biological Samples for Research primarily articulate consent at the individual participant level, emphasising voluntariness, language accessibility, and ethics committee oversight. Although the Guidelines acknowledge cultural sensitivity and vulnerable populations, they do not expressly establish a parallel framework for community-level or collective consent in Indigenous settings. Consequently, research practices that obtain individual written consent and institutional ethics approval may achieve formal compliance while still generating ethical tensions where communal decision-making traditions and shared identity remain central.

This individual-centric orientation contrasts with several international ethical instruments, including the CIOMS International Ethical Guidelines (CIOMS, 2016) and the OECD Guidelines on Human Biobanks (OECD, 2009), which acknowledge that in culturally distinct or Indigenous contexts, community consultation and collective deliberation may ethically complement individual consent. Such instruments do not displace personal autonomy but recognise that ethical legitimacy may, in some societies, also derive from communal participation and shared decision-making.

(B) INFORMED CONSENT AS A CULTURALLY SITUATED PROCESS

Standard written consent forms, even when translated into Bahasa Malaysia, may not adequately convey complex scientific concepts such as genomic sequencing, long-term biobanking, or data sovereignty. For communities with strong oral traditions or differing epistemological frameworks, biological samples may be perceived not merely as personal property but as extensions of ancestry, land, and spiritual continuity.

Accordingly, obtaining a meaningful consent from under-represented populations requires **contextual translation**, participatory dialogue, and verification of understanding, rather than reliance on standardised documents alone.

(C) RISKS OF CULTURAL MISAPPROPRIATION AND BIOCOLONIAL NARRATIVES

The collection of biological materials without culturally grounded consultation can be interpreted as extractive or exploitative, particularly where benefits do not visibly return to the community. This risk is not purely symbolic; it may contribute to mistrust, identity stereotyping, or the perception that Indigenous knowledge systems are being commodified.

(D) ETHICAL ENGAGEMENT WITH INDIGENOUS COMMUNITIES

To promote culturally respectful and ethically robust biobanking practices in Indigenous contexts, several practical measures may be adopted:

1. Community-Level Consultation Prior to Individual Recruitment Engage elders, councils, and representative groups through dialogue rather than relying solely on a single leader's approval.

2. Co-Developed Consent Materials Use culturally adapted language, oral explanations, and participatory visuals rather than standardised legal forms.

3. Recognition of Collective Limitations and Refusal Rights Allow communities to set boundaries on storage duration, international transfer, or commercial use.

4. Use of Cultural Mediators or Liaison Officers Collaboration with Indigenous NGOs or advisors can align research practices with customary expectations.

5. Ongoing Communication and Feedback Loops Treat consent as a continuous relationship, updating communities on findings and data usage over time.

Key Takeaways

- **Individual consent alone may be ethically incomplete in Indigenous contexts.**
  Where identity, heritage, and biological materials are understood collectively, community consultation may be necessary alongside personal agreement to ensure respectful and legitimate participation.
- **Cultural translation must extend beyond language.**
  Providing forms in a national language does not automatically ensure understanding; ethical consent requires explaining scientific concepts in locally meaningful and culturally resonant terms.
- **Regulatory compliance does not always equal ethical adequacy.**
  Obtaining written consent and ethics approval may satisfy formal requirements, yet tensions can arise when institutional processes do not align with communal decision-making traditions.
- **Reciprocity and respectful engagement strengthen legitimacy.**
  Visible community benefits, transparent communication, and continued dialogue help prevent perceptions of extractive or one-sided research practices.

2.5 Concluding Reflections

This chapter has examined informed consent in Malaysian biobanking, not merely as a procedural requirement but as a multidimensional ethical, legal, and social practice. Consent in the biobank context extends beyond the signing of a form or the fulfilment of institutional requirements; it functions as a continuing communicative relationship shaped by technological change, cultural diversity, and evolving public expectations. Although Malaysia does not yet have a single comprehensive statute dedicated exclusively to biobanking, a layered framework exists through data protection legislation, national ethical guidelines, professional standards, and institutional ethics review. These instruments establish important legal and procedural thresholds, yet ethical adequacy ultimately depends on how these standards are interpreted and enacted in practice.

The analyses in this chapter demonstrate that informed consent carries both individual and institutional significance. At the individual level, it safeguards autonomy, dignity, and informational control. At the institutional level, it operates as a mechanism of legitimacy, enabling research systems to maintain public confidence and voluntary participation. This dual character explains why weaknesses in consent practices often generate consequences that extend beyond personal dissatisfaction; they may influence institutional credibility, research sustainability, and societal acceptance of biomedical innovation. In the era of genomic research and large-scale data sharing, these implications become even more pronounced, as biological materials and associated data may circulate across borders and persist long after initial collection.

The three case studies illustrate how ethical challenges emerge in distinct yet interconnected ways. The first case underscores the procedural dimension of consent, revealing how ambiguous language and over-generalised disclosure can result in formal compliance without substantive understanding. The second case highlights the influence of religious and cultural frameworks, demonstrating that moral comfort and ethical acceptance are shaped not only by information but also by belief systems, authority dynamics, and communicative style. The third case shifts attention to collective identity and communal decision-making, showing that individualistic consent models may not fully capture the ethical realities of societies in which knowledge, heritage, and biological materials are understood relationally rather than purely personally.

Overall, these scenarios reveal that informed consent in Malaysia operates at the intersection of law, ethics, culture, and community life. Effective consent is not achieved solely through comprehensive documentation but through meaningful dialogue, contextual explanation, and sensitivity to social structures that influence how participation is interpreted. Transparency regarding commercial collaboration, accessibility of language, and respectful engagement with communal norms do not merely enhance compliance;

they strengthen the moral legitimacy of research activities and help prevent perceptions of exploitation or exclusion. In this sense, ethical consent is less about eliminating all uncertainty than it is about ensuring that participants are meaningfully aware of its scope and implications.

From a governance perspective, the chapter also highlights the importance of adaptive oversight mechanisms. Institutional Review Boards, national ethical guidelines, and professional codes serve as critical bridges between abstract principles and operational practice. Their role extends beyond approving consent templates to fostering cultures of accountability, inclusivity, and continuous ethical reflection. As Malaysian biobanking continues to expand through international collaboration and technological advancement, the interpretive and supervisory functions of these bodies will become increasingly central to balancing scientific progress with participant protection.

Ultimately, informed consent in biobanking should be understood as a dynamic ethical infrastructure rather than as a static legal formality. Its strength lies in its capacity to accommodate diversity of language, belief, and social organisation while preserving core principles of autonomy, fairness, and transparency. For a multi-ethnic and multicultural society such as Malaysia, this adaptability is not simply desirable but essential. Strengthening consent practices therefore involves more than regulatory refinement; it requires sustained attention to communication, cultural awareness, and institutional trustworthiness. By recognising consent as both a personal right and a relational social practice, Malaysian biobank governance can continue to evolve in a manner that aligns scientific advancement with ethical integrity and public confidence.

References

Abdul Aziz, M. F., & Mohd Yusof, A. N. (2019). Can dynamic consent facilitate the protection of biomedical big data in biobanking in Malaysia? *Asian Bioethics Review*, *11*(2), 209–222. https://pmc.ncbi.nlm.nih.gov/articles/PMC7747242/

Byrnes, E. V. (2025). *Consent to biobank research: Could having justified trust substitute for having substantial understanding, and still provide ethically valid consent for research participation?* University of Pittsburgh.

Fitzpatrick, E. F., Martiniuk, A. L., D'Antoine, H., Oscar, J., Carter, M., & Elliott, E. J. (2016). Seeking consent for research with indigenous communities: A systematic review. *BMC Medical Ethics*, *17*(1), 65. https://doi.org/10.1186/s12910-016-0139-8

Garrison, N. A., Carroll, S. R., & Hudson, M. (2020). Entwined processes: Rescripting consent and strengthening governance in genomics research with indigenous communities. *Journal of Law, Medicine & Ethics*, *48*(1), 218–220. https://doi.org/10.1177/1073110520917020

Garrison, N. A., Hudson, M., Ballantyne, L. L., Garba, I., Martinez, A., Taualii, M., Arbour, L., Caron, N. R., & Rainie, S. C. (2019). Genomic research through an indigenous lens: Understanding the expectations. *Annual Review of Genomics and Human Genetics*, *20*(1), 495–517.

Hartanti, W., Wahdi, A. E., Prasetiawati, T., Izhati, Q. A., & Fachiroh, J. (2025). Developing informed consent for academic hospital-based biobank modeling: An experience from Indonesia. *Biopreservation and Biobanking*, *23*(3), 186–194. https://journals.sagepub.com/doi/10.1089/bio.2024.0001?url_ver=Z39.88-2003&rfr_id=ori:rid:crossref.org&rfr_dat=cr_pub%20%200pubmed

International Ethical Guidelines for Health-Related Research Involving Humans. (2016). CIOMS.

Lay, W., Gasparini, L., Siero, W., & Hughes, E. K. (2025). A rapid review of the benefits and challenges of dynamic consent. *Research Ethics*, *21*(1), 180–202.

Lee, Y. S., Garrido, N. L. B., Lord, G., Maggio, Z. A., & Khomtchouk, B. B. (2025). Ethical considerations for biobanks serving underrepresented populations. *Bioethics*, *39*(3), 240–249. https://onlinelibrary.wiley.com/doi/pdfdirect/10.1111/bioe.13381?download=true

OECD Guidelines and Human Biobanks and Genetic Research Databases. (2009).

Tone-Pah-Hote, T., & Redvers, N. (2022). The commercialization of biospecimens from indigenous Peoples: A scoping review of benefit-sharing. *Frontiers in Medicine (Lausanne)*, *9*, 978826. https://doi.org/10.3389/fmed.2022.978826

Tsosie, K. S., Yracheta, J. M., & Dickenson, D. (2019). Overvaluing individual consent ignores risks to tribal participants. *Nature Reviews Genetics*, *20*(9), 497–498. https://doi.org/10.1038/s41576-019-0161-z

Universal Declaration on Bioethics and Human Rights. (2006). UNESCO.

3 Privacy and Confidentiality in Biobanking

3.1 The Role of Privacy and Confidentiality in Biobanking

In the biobanking sector, privacy and confidentiality constitute foundational safeguards that protect individuals' sensitive personal and health-related information. Biobanks routinely collect, store, and analyse biological samples alongside identifiable or potentially identifiable data over extended periods, often for unspecified future research. Within such long-term and data-intensive infrastructures, privacy and confidentiality are not merely administrative obligations but function as conditions of ethical legitimacy and public trust. Empirical research consistently demonstrates that willingness to participate in biobank initiatives is closely linked to confidence in institutional data-protection practices and perceived respect for informational boundaries (Pullman et al., 2012; Siminoff et al., 2017).

Biological samples, particularly genetic and genomic material, contain highly personal and enduring information. Unlike many other forms of personal data, genetic information is inherently relational and predictive. It can reveal disease predispositions, ancestry, familial relationships, and characteristics that may carry social stigma or discrimination risks. Unauthorised disclosure therefore implicates not only the individual donor but also, in some instances, biological relatives and communities. The ethical gravity of privacy breaches in biobanking is thus amplified when compared with ordinary medical record disclosures, as the potential harms extend to discrimination in employment, insurance exclusion, social stigmatisation, and erosion of personal dignity.

Confidentiality in the biobanking context refers to the continuing obligation of custodians, researchers, and affiliated institutions to prevent unauthorised identification, access, or disclosure of participant data. This obligation is operationalised through layered safeguards such as coding or pseudonymisation, encryption protocols, controlled-access databases, audit trails, and contractual restrictions in data-sharing arrangements. Importantly, confidentiality does not imply absolute secrecy; rather, it requires that any disclosure be lawful, proportionate, and transparently governed within the parameters

DOI: 10.4324/9781003745785-3

communicated to participants and reviewed by ethics committees (CIOMS, 2016, Guideline 11; OECD, 2009).

The ethical obligation to protect privacy in biobanking is closely linked to, but conceptually distinct from, autonomy. Although informed consent authorises the initial collection and specified uses of data, privacy and confidentiality govern the ongoing stewardship of that data throughout its lifecycle. International bioethics instruments increasingly recognise this distinction, emphasising that data protection duties persist even where consent has been validly obtained (CIOMS, 2016, Art. 9; UNESCO, 2006).

Beyond ethical imperatives, robust confidentiality protections also serve an instrumental function. Public confidence in biobanks is directly correlated with perceptions of institutional responsibility and transparency. Where participants trust that their personal and genetic information will be treated with care, they are more likely to contribute samples, thereby strengthening dataset diversity and research validity. Conversely, widely publicised breaches or opaque data-sharing practices risk undermining the long-term sustainability of national biobanking initiatives, a concern echoed in Malaysian policy discussions on national biorepository governance (Working Committee for the Establishment of the National Biorepository Policy for Malaysia, 2023).

3.2 Legal and Ethical Standards in Malaysia

In Malaysia, privacy and confidentiality in biobanking are governed through a multi-layered regulatory architecture comprising statutory data-protection legislation, sector-specific health laws, ministerial guidelines, and internationally recognised ethical frameworks. Malaysian governance relies on the interaction between these instruments, which collectively impose obligations on institutions handling biological materials and associated data.

Ethically, Malaysian biomedical research practice is strongly influenced by international standards such as the Declaration of Helsinki, the CIOMS International Ethical Guidelines, and the UNESCO Universal Declaration on Bioethics and Human Rights, all of which explicitly articulate duties to safeguard personal data and respect confidentiality. These international norms are frequently incorporated into domestic ethics review processes and institutional standard operating procedures.

3.2.1 Ethical Standards for Biomedical and Biobank-Related Research

At the national level, ethical governance of human biological materials is primarily guided by Ministry of Health instruments such as the Malaysian Guidelines on the Use of Human Biological Samples for Research (2nd ed., 2025), which explicitly lists Privacy and Confidentiality as a core guiding principle. The Guidelines emphasise that institutions must adopt data-management systems that ensure secure storage, restricted access, and traceable data-handling practices, while balancing transparency with the protection of participant identity (Malaysia Ministry of Health, 2025)

Similarly, the Malaysian Guideline for Good Clinical Practice (GCP) embeds confidentiality obligations within broader duties of data integrity, subject protection, and ethics committee oversight. Although originally designed for clinical trials, its principles are frequently applied by research ethics committees reviewing biobank-related protocols, particularly in relation to secure record-keeping and controlled data access (Health, 2018).

The ethical expectations reflected in these guidelines mirror international norms:

Confidentiality

Researchers and custodial institutions are required to ensure that identifiable information is protected through anonymisation or pseudonymisation wherever feasible, and that disclosure occurs only under authorised and ethically reviewed conditions (CIOMS, 2016, Guideline 11).

Respect for Persons and Informational Control

Detailed consent theory is addressed in earlier chapters, but it is relevant here insofar as participants must be informed of the privacy safeguards, potential data-sharing arrangements, and limits of confidentiality, particularly in cross-border collaborations.

Beneficence, Non-Maleficence, and Justice

These principles extend to privacy management by requiring institutions to minimise informational risks, prevent misuse or commercial exploitation without disclosure, and ensure that vulnerable populations are not disproportionately exposed to confidentiality breaches.

The Malaysian Code of Responsible Conduct in Research further reinforces these obligations by framing data stewardship and confidentiality as elements of research integrity and institutional accountability (Council, 2020).

3.3 Data Protection Legislation and Its Implications for Biobanks

Beyond ethical guidance, Malaysia's statutory framework provides legally enforceable standards governing the processing of personal data, including health and genetic information. The Personal Data Protection Act 2010 (PDPA) and its subsequent amendments form the central legal instrument regulating the collection, processing, storage, and disclosure of personal data in commercial transactions ("Personal Data Protection Act", 2010). Although the PDPA's formal application to government bodies is limited, its principles exert substantial normative influence across public and private research institutions.

3.3.1 Overview of the Personal Data Protection Act 2010 and 2024 Amendments

The PDPA establishes a set of Personal Data Protection Principles that are directly relevant to biobanks handling identifiable or coded biological data. Health and genetic information fall within the category of sensitive personal data, thereby attracting heightened safeguards. Key provisions with practical implications for biobanking operations include:

Consent and Notice

Biobanks must obtain explicit and informed consent for data processing and provide clear notice of purposes, access arrangements, and retention practices.

Data Minimisation and Purpose Limitation

Only data necessary for the stated research objectives should be collected, and secondary use must remain within ethically reviewed parameters.

Security Principle

Institutions are required to implement "practical steps" to protect personal data from loss, misuse, unauthorised access, or disclosure. In biobanking, this extends to encrypted databases, tiered access permissions, and secure physical storage of samples.

Access and Correction Rights

Participants retain statutory rights to request access to their personal data and seek corrections where inaccuracies arise.

Cross-Border Data Transfer Controls

International data sharing must occur only where recipient jurisdictions provide adequate protection or where contractual safeguards ensure equivalent standards.

The Personal Data Protection (Amendment) Act 2024 strengthens these protections by introducing enhanced accountability mechanisms, updated terminology from "data user" to "data controller", and expanded recognition of biometric and sensitive data categories, thereby reinforcing the legal expectation that genomic and health-related data receive stringent protection ("Personal Data Protection (Amendment) Act", 2024).

3.3.2 Implications for Biobanks

For biobanks operating within Malaysia's research ecosystem, the PDPA and related guidelines translate into several operational obligations:

Compliance-Driven Consent and Record Management

Institutions must maintain verifiable documentation of participant permissions and ensure that consent preferences are accurately reflected in data-access systems.

Enhanced Technical and Organisational Safeguards

Security measures must encompass digital encryption, physical sample protection, and administrative access controls. International best-practice literature emphasises that privacy protection is most effective when embedded into system design rather than applied retrospectively (OECD, 2009; Takai-Igarashi et al., 2017).

Cross-Jurisdictional Data Governance

International collaborations require harmonisation of contractual agreements and ethical approvals to ensure equivalent confidentiality standards.

Breach Notification and Remedial Measures

Where data breaches occur, institutions are expected to notify relevant authorities and affected participants promptly and to implement corrective mechanisms that restore trust and prevent recurrence.

Overall, these legal and ethical instruments position privacy and confidentiality not as peripheral compliance tasks but as core governance pillars within Malaysia's evolving biobanking landscape.

3.4 Case Studies

3.4.1 Case Study 1: The Breach of Confidentiality

Case Narrative

A Malaysian biobank entered into a collaborative research project with an international medical research institute to investigate genetic markers associated with rare diseases prevalent within Southeast Asian populations. The collaboration required cross-border sharing of datasets comprising coded genetic sequences and accompanying clinical metadata. The biobank intended to transmit only anonymised data in accordance with the research protocol and the data-sharing agreement.

During dataset preparation, however, a technical oversight resulted in residual identifiers, including partial dates of birth, ethnicity markers, and diagnostic codes, remaining embedded within the dataset. Although direct identifiers had been removed, the retained variables were sufficiently granular to permit re-identification through data linkage techniques. Upon receipt, the international research team detected the residual identifiers and notified the Malaysian partner institution. Before corrective measures were fully implemented, several participants became aware of the incident through informal channels, prompting public concern regarding misuse, discrimination, and reputational harm.

The incident did not involve deliberate disclosure or commercial exploitation. Nevertheless, it constituted a confidentiality breach arising from inadequate de-identification controls and insufficient pre-transfer audit procedures. The scenario raises intersecting ethical and legal questions regarding institutional data stewardship, cross-border data governance, and the adequacy of technical safeguards in biobank infrastructures.

Commentary

(A) STATUTORY DATA PROTECTION OBLIGATIONS UNDER MALAYSIAN LAW

The central legal instrument engaged in this scenario is the Personal Data Protection Act 2010 (PDPA) ("Personal Data Protection Act", 2010). The breach, although technical in origin rather than malicious, illustrates how inadequate de-identification controls may nonetheless constitute a governance lapse with tangible consequences for both participants and institutions.

From the participants' perspective, the exposure of genetic and health-related information generates risks that are not merely informational but also socially consequential. Genetic data is predictive and relational; its inadvertent disclosure may enable profiling, insurance discrimination, or reputational harm extending to family members. Such risks fall squarely within the protective intent of the PDPA's Security Principle (Section 9), which obliges data controllers to take "practical steps" to prevent unauthorised access, disclosure, or misuse. The presence of residual identifiers suggests that the biobank's security measures were procedurally insufficient rather than technologically absent, highlighting that compliance requires systematic verification processes, not simply encryption or password controls.

Institutionally, the reputational harm to the biobank reflects the PDPA's broader Accountability orientation, reinforced by the Personal Data Protection (Amendment) Act 2024, which strengthens breach-notification expectations and controller responsibilities ("Personal Data Protection (Amendment) Act", 2024). The incident demonstrates that legal compliance in data protection is inseparable from public trust; regulatory scrutiny and diminished participant confidence are not collateral effects but foreseeable outcomes of inadequate safeguards.

The Disclosure Principle (Section 8 PDPA) is also implicated. Even where participants had consented to international collaboration, such consent was premised on the understanding that only anonymised data would be shared. The issue therefore lies not in the absence of consent but in the misalignment between represented and actual data conditions, which undermines informational fairness.

Furthermore, Section 129 PDPA on cross-border data transfer assumes that data leaving the jurisdiction has already been appropriately de-identified or otherwise safeguarded. Residual identifiers complicate adequacy assessments and increase the regulatory exposure of both the transferring and receiving institutions, thereby illustrating how confidentiality breaches in collaborative research create shared accountability rather than unilateral fault.

(B) MINISTERIAL AND PROFESSIONAL ETHICAL INSTRUMENTS

Beyond statutory obligations, the incident reveals tensions between aspirational ethical standards and operational practice. The Malaysian Guidelines on the Use of Human Biological Samples for Research expressly identify Privacy and Confidentiality as Guiding Principle 7, requiring secure storage, restricted access, and traceable data-handling mechanisms (Malaysia Ministry of Health, 2025). The technical oversight in this case demonstrates that compliance with these expectations depends less on policy declarations and more on verifiable pre-transfer audits and role-based access controls.

Similarly, the Malaysian Guideline for Good Clinical Practice (GCP), although oriented toward interventional trials, embeds confidentiality obligations within its requirements for subject record protection and controlled data access (Health, 2018). Ethics committees reviewing biobank collaborations frequently apply these standards by analogy, reinforcing the expectation that participant confidentiality persists beyond the clinical setting and into long-term data repositories.

The Malaysian Code of Responsible Conduct in Research (MCRCR) further frames confidentiality as an element of institutional research integrity, underscoring that responsibility for secure data stewardship rests with organisations rather than solely with individual investigators (Council, 2020). In this sense, the breach represents not merely an individual lapse but a systemic shortfall in governance architecture.

(C) INTERNATIONAL NORMATIVE ANCHORS

International instruments commonly relied upon in Malaysian ethics review processes reinforce the continuing nature of confidentiality obligations. The CIOMS International Ethical Guidelines 2016, particularly Guidelines 11 and 12, emphasise that safeguarding biological materials and related data extends beyond initial consent and requires ongoing minimisation of re-identification risks (CIOMS, 2016). The Declaration of Helsinki similarly mandates that every precaution be taken to protect research participants' privacy and confidentiality, while the OECD Guidelines on Human Biobanks and Genetic Research Databases frame custodianship and layered security as institutional duties rather than as discretionary safeguards.

Collectively, these instruments underscore that anonymisation is a risk-mitigation strategy, not a definitive guarantee of anonymity, and must therefore be supported by procedural verification and governance oversight.

Key Takeaways

Anonymisation and pseudonymisation reduce risk but do not eliminate re-identification possibilities, particularly when datasets contain indirect identifiers such as ethnicity, rare diagnoses, or granular demographic variables. Continuous verification mechanisms are therefore essential.

- **Confidentiality obligations are ongoing, not exhausted by consent.** Even where participants have consented to data sharing, institutions remain bound by continuing duties under the PDPA Security and Disclosure Principles and by ethical guidelines requiring sustained data stewardship.
- **Cross-border collaborations generate shared accountability.** Both sending and receiving institutions bear responsibility for safeguarding participant identity, particularly under PDPA cross-border transfer provisions and CIOMS data protection expectations.
- **Technical safeguards must be paired with procedural controls.** Encryption, firewalls, and access controls are insufficient without pre-transfer audits, identifier-screening protocols, and role-based authorisation systems, as emphasised in Malaysian Human Biological Samples Guidelines Principle 7.
- **Institutional reputation is inseparable from data governance.** Loss of participant trust can have longer-term implications than regulatory penalties, affecting recruitment, funding, and international collaboration prospects.
- **Breach response transparency is itself an ethical obligation.** Prompt notification to affected participants and regulatory authorities, consistent with the PDPA Amendment 2024 accountability framework, is integral to restoring confidence and demonstrating governance integrity.

- **Privacy protection should operate on a "privacy-by-design" model.** Confidentiality safeguards must be embedded within the infrastructure and workflow of biobanks rather than applied reactively after incidents occur.

3.4.2 Case Study 2: Cross-Border Anxiety and Digital Re-Identification

Case Narrative

Mr. Lim, a 55-year-old retired teacher of Chinese Buddhist background residing in Penang, consented to participate in a university-led cardiovascular genetics study forming part of a regional collaboration with institutions in Singapore, Taiwan, and South Korea. His DNA sample and associated clinical records were stored in a Malaysian biobank, with the understanding that data might be anonymised and shared for research purposes.

Two years later, Mr. Lim encountered public reports describing how anonymised genetic datasets could be re-identified through online genealogy platforms, surname inference, and data-linkage techniques. Upon contacting the biobank, he learned that his coded genetic data had indeed been shared internationally under an approved data-sharing agreement.

Mr. Lim expressed his concern regarding the irreversible and intergenerational nature of DNA disclosure. Beyond personal privacy, his anxiety centred on familial reputation, ancestral continuity, and the possibility that genetic data might circulate in commercial or defence-related datasets beyond his knowledge. Although no actual re-identification had occurred, the perceived loss of informational control generated distrust and emotional distress, illustrating how confidentiality risks in genomics extend beyond demonstrable breaches to encompass anticipatory and cultural harms.

Commentary

(A) DIGITAL RE-IDENTIFICATION AND THE LIMITS OF ANONYMISATION

Technological developments in big-data analytics, genealogy platforms, and surname inference have substantially narrowed the practical distinction between "anonymised" and "re-identifiable" genomic data. Even where direct identifiers are removed, combinations of demographic variables, rare disease markers, or lineage-specific surnames may enable triangulation.

Within the Malaysian legal context, this risk engages the PDPA Security Principle (Section 9) and Sensitive Personal Data provisions (Section 40), which require data controllers to adopt safeguards proportionate to the sensitivity and identifiability of the data ("Personal Data Protection Act", 2010).

The issue is not that anonymisation is impermissible, but that representing anonymisation as absolute privacy protection may create a misleading expectation of irreversibility. The Personal Data Protection (Amendment) Act 2024 further strengthens accountability expectations, signalling that controllers must anticipate foreseeable technological re-identification risks rather than rely on static de-identification assumptions ("Personal Data Protection (Amendment) Act", 2024).

International ethical standards similarly recognise this limitation. CIOMS Guidelines 11 and 12 emphasise that confidentiality duties persist even where identifiers have been removed, and that governance mechanisms must evolve alongside technological capabilities (CIOMS, 2016). In practical terms, anonymisation operates as risk mitigation rather than as risk elimination.

(B) CULTURAL CONCEPTIONS OF GENETIC INFORMATION AND RELATIONAL PRIVACY

Mr. Lim's concerns illustrate that genetic data is not universally perceived as individual property. Within many East Asian cultural contexts, DNA is intertwined with notions of lineage continuity, ancestral respect, and collective dignity. The ethical implications of disclosure therefore extend beyond the individual participant to family members and future generations.

Although Malaysian statutes such as the PDPA adopt an individual-centric data subject model, ministerial and ethical guidelines increasingly recognise relational dimensions of biological materials. The Malaysian Guidelines on the Use of Human Biological Samples for Research identify Privacy and Confidentiality as Guiding Principle 7, implicitly requiring culturally responsive governance where data-handling practices may affect familial or communal identities (Malaysia Ministry of Health, 2025). The concern here is not legal ownership of DNA, but interpretive legitimacy – whether governance structures adequately acknowledge that confidentiality failures may produce collective reputational harm even in the absence of direct identification.

(C) CROSS-BORDER DATA GOVERNANCE AND COMMUNICATION OBLIGATIONS

The international sharing of genomic data introduces additional layers of legal and ethical responsibility. Under Section 129 PDPA, personal data transferred outside Malaysia must be subject to adequate protection or equivalent contractual safeguards ("Personal Data Protection Act", 2010). However, adequacy is not solely a legal question; it is also a matter of participant perception and transparency.

Where participants are not clearly informed of the jurisdictions involved, the identities of collaborating institutions, or the practical limits of de-identification, the resulting anxiety may arise even without demonstrable misuse. The ethical concern therefore lies in risk communication rather than regulatory non-compliance. Ministerial instruments such as the Malaysian Guideline for Good Clinical Practice (GCP) reinforce expectations of clarity in subject information and data-handling disclosures, particularly where international collaborations are involved (Health, 2018).

(D) STATIC CONSENT MODELS AND ONGOING DATA STEWARDSHIP

Mr. Lim's experience also exposes the structural limits of one-time consent in long-term genomic research. Although Malaysian law does not mandate dynamic consent systems, both the **MCRCR** and CIOMS guidelines emphasise continuing responsibilities in data stewardship and participant engagement. The ethical shortfall is therefore less about invalid consent and more about **insufficient mechanisms for ongoing participant reassurance and agency**. In genomic contexts where risks evolve alongside technology, confidentiality governance must be iterative rather than static.

Key Takeaways

- **Anonymisation is technologically contingent.**
  It should be communicated as a risk-reduction measure, not a guarantee of irreversibility, particularly in genomic datasets where lineage markers enable triangulation.
- **Security obligations include anticipatory risk assessment.**
  Under the PDPA Security Principle and 2024 amendments, institutions are expected to anticipate foreseeable re-identification techniques rather than rely solely on traditional de-identification methods.
- **Genetic confidentiality may carry relational and cultural dimensions.**
  Data governance frameworks should acknowledge that reputational or spiritual harms may extend to families, not merely individual participants.
- **Cross-border transparency is an ethical requirement, not merely a contractual formality.**
  Participants should be informed of collaborating jurisdictions, applicable protections, and the realistic limits of confidentiality safeguards.
- **Static consent is insufficient in evolving genomic research environments.**
  Although not legally mandated, mechanisms enabling ongoing participant engagement or consent review enhance trust and align with international ethical expectations.
- **Perceived loss of control can constitute ethical harm even without actual breach.**
  Confidentiality governance must therefore address psychological and cultural reassurance alongside technical compliance.

3.4.3 Case Study 3: Posthumous Privacy and Cultural Sensitivity

Case Narrative

Mrs. Shanti Devi, a 63-year-old Indian woman of Hindu background from Ipoh, contributed blood and tissue samples to a university biobank investigating genetic predispositions to breast and ovarian cancers. Motivated by intergenerational benefit, she provided broad consent permitting future research use of her samples.

Following her passing, her family discovered that her biological materials had been included in a secondary study on genetic biomarkers associated with schizophrenia and bipolar disorder conducted in collaboration with a European pharmaceutical entity. Although the data had been anonymised, the family expressed deep discomfort upon learning that her samples were linked to psychiatric research, an area associated with social stigma within the local community. Their concern did not stem from opposition to scientific inquiry per se, but from perceived reputational implications, spiritual unease regarding posthumous bodily use, and the absence of explicit disclosure that her samples might be repurposed for mental-health or commercially affiliated studies. The family contemplated raising the matter before the hospital's ethics committee.

Commentary

(A) POSTHUMOUS PRIVACY AND SECONDARY USE OF BIOLOGICAL MATERIALS

Unlike conventional medical records, biological samples retain enduring informational and symbolic value even after death. Malaysian statutory law does not expressly recognise a standalone "posthumous privacy right", yet several regulatory instruments indirectly govern post-death use of bodily materials. The Human Tissues Act 1974 permits removal and use of parts of a deceased person's body for medical education or research where prior consent exists or where no objection is known, thereby establishing the legal permissibility of posthumous research use ("Human Tissue Act", 1974).

However, legal permissibility does not resolve ethical adequacy. Where consent is framed broadly without explicit reference to secondary or commercially affiliated research, families may perceive a divergence between the donor's altruistic intent and subsequent research trajectories. The issue here is not unlawful use, but expectation misalignment – a governance gap between legal authorisation and socially acceptable stewardship.

The Malaysian Guidelines on the Use of Human Biological Samples for Research emphasise that custodianship of samples entails responsibilities extending beyond collection, including respectful handling, culturally sensitive communication, and ethical oversight in secondary use decisions (Malaysia Ministry of Health, 2025). Although anonymisation protects individual identity, it does not neutralise symbolic or familial concerns regarding the nature of the research domain itself.

(B) MENTAL HEALTH RESEARCH AND SOCIAL STIGMA

This case highlights that confidentiality risks may arise not from identification but from associative stigma. In many South Asian and Southeast Asian contexts, psychiatric illness remains socially sensitive, with implications for marriage prospects, social standing, and communal perceptions of familial honour. Even anonymised inclusion in mental-health genomics research may generate distress where families interpret participation as symbolic association rather than data abstraction.

International ethical standards acknowledge that certain research domains warrant heightened sensitivity. CIOMS Guidelines 4 and 11 underscore the need to consider potential social harms arising from the use of biological materials, including stigma and group-based discrimination (CIOMS, 2016). The concern therefore extends beyond informational privacy to reputational and communal dignity, particularly where research subjects are deceased and unable to clarify their intent.

(C) RELIGIOUS AND CULTURAL INTERPRETATIONS OF BODILY INTEGRITY

Hindu ethical perspectives do not categorically prohibit tissue donation or posthumous research. Nonetheless, many adherents emphasise ritual purity, respectful bodily treatment, and symbolic continuity of the deceased's legacy. The discomfort expressed by Mrs. Shanti Devi's family reflects not doctrinal prohibition but interpretive sensitivity – the belief that bodily materials should not be associated with domains perceived as dishonourable or spiritually discordant.

Malaysian ministerial instruments do not mandate religious consultation, yet they explicitly require a culturally responsive approach in biomedical research, as stated in the Malaysian Guidelines on the Use of Human Biological Samples for Research – this approach is particularly vital in Malaysia's multi-faith society. Moreover, the absence of explicit statutory prohibition does not negate the ethical expectation that custodians exercise discretion and contextual awareness in approving secondary uses involving socially sensitive topics.

(D) LEGAL SUFFICIENCY VERSUS ETHICAL ACCEPTABILITY

The central tension in this case lies between legal sufficiency and ethical legitimacy. Broad consent may satisfy minimal statutory thresholds, especially where anonymisation is maintained. Nevertheless, ethical governance demands anticipatory consideration of how secondary research domains may be perceived by surviving family members or communities.

The Malaysian Code of Responsible Conduct in Research (MCRCR) frames data and sample stewardship as an institutional responsibility grounded in integrity, transparency, and accountability (Council, 2020). From this perspective, ethical review boards are expected to assess not only regulatory compliance but also contextual appropriateness, particularly where research domains intersect with social stigma or cultural sensitivity.

Key Takeaways

- **Legal authorisation does not exhaust ethical responsibility.**
  The Human Tissues Act 1974 permits posthumous research use, but ethical legitimacy depends on alignment between donor expectations and secondary research domains.
- **Anonymisation does not eliminate associative or symbolic harms.**
  Even where identity is protected, research involving stigmatised domains such as mental health may generate reputational or communal distress.
- **Broad consent requires contextual interpretation in secondary use.**
  Ethical oversight bodies should evaluate whether new research trajectories remain consistent with the donor's probable intent and cultural milieu.
- **Posthumous use engages relational and cultural dimensions of privacy.**
  Families may perceive biological materials as extensions of legacy or lineage rather than as neutral data artefacts.
- **Ethics committees play a mediating role between legality and social acceptability.**
  Review processes should incorporate cultural sensitivity and potential stigma assessments rather than relying solely on statutory compliance.
- **Transparent communication mitigates posthumous distrust.**
  Although next-of-kin consent is not legally mandated, proactive disclosure regarding secondary or commercially affiliated research can preserve institutional credibility and community confidence.

3.4.4 Case Study 4: Privacy, Community Sovereignty, and the Orang Asli Context

Case Narrative

Following the completion of a previously consented national genomic surveillance study, researchers from a Malaysian university, in collaboration with an international bioinformatics firm, proceeded to analyse, categorise, and store genomic data derived from Temiar Orang Asli villagers in northern Perak. The subsequent phase of the project involved long-term database integration, metadata classification, and secondary analytical use of collected DNA sequences rather than fresh sample collection. Although initial engagement with the *tok batin* (village head) and individual consent documentation had occurred during the data-gathering stage, no further consultation was undertaken regarding downstream storage, cross-border processing, or extended data retention.

Months later, Indigenous advocacy organisations raised concerns that while personal identifiers had been removed, descriptors such as tribal classification, language group, and geographic origin remained embedded in the dataset. These metadata elements rendered the community collectively identifiable as a distinct genetic subgroup within international databases. There had been no structured discussion with the community concerning how such categorisation might affect their collective identity, nor any agreement regarding benefit-sharing, commercial partnerships, or long-term data governance. The episode generated public debate on whether anonymisation sufficiently protects Indigenous privacy and whether genomic classification risks reinforcing stereotyping or marginalisation despite formal consent having been obtained at the initial stage.

Commentary

(A) COLLECTIVE PRIVACY AND THE LIMITS OF INDIVIDUAL DATA PROTECTION MODELS

This scenario illustrates a structural tension between individual-centric privacy frameworks and collective identity-based harms. Malaysian statutory data protection law, particularly the Personal Data Protection Act 2010 (PDPA), conceptualises privacy through the lens of an individual "data subject" ("Personal Data Protection Act", 2010). This model provides baseline protection for identifiable personal information, but it does not explicitly recognise collective reputational or cultural harm arising from group identifiability.

In Indigenous contexts such as the Orang Asli communities, genetic information is often regarded not merely as personal data but as shared heritage, intertwined with ancestry, spirituality, and communal dignity. The removal of names and identity card numbers may therefore satisfy formal anonymisation criteria without addressing deeper concerns regarding group representation and symbolic ownership. Ministerial instruments such as the Malaysian Guidelines on the Use of Human Biological Samples for Research implicitly acknowledge this relational dimension by emphasising respectful handling, transparency, and culturally appropriate engagement in secondary use decisions (Malaysia Ministry of Health, 2025).

(B) METADATA, CULTURAL TRACEABILITY, AND RE-IDENTIFICATION RISKS

The continued attachment of tribal and linguistic descriptors demonstrates the distinction between personal anonymisation and cultural traceability. Even where direct identifiers are removed, metadata may function as indirect identifiers capable of revealing a community's presence within a dataset. In small or distinct populations, such traceability can facilitate stereotyping or essentialising narratives that affect social standing or policy perceptions.

From a legal standpoint, this engages the PDPA's Security Principle (Section 9), which obliges data controllers to adopt safeguards proportionate to the sensitivity and identifiability of data ("Personal Data Protection Act", 2010). Yet the principle is framed primarily in technical terms and does not explicitly address collective identifiability. International ethical standards, particularly CIOMS Guidelines 4 and 11, extend the analysis by cautioning against group-based harms and social stigmatisation arising from biological research (CIOMS, 2016). The ethical concern therefore lies not solely in personal privacy breaches, but rather in the social consequences of collective categorisation.

(C) DATA SOVEREIGNTY AND POST-CONSENT GOVERNANCE

The advocacy response reflects a broader global discourse on Indigenous data sovereignty – the principle that communities retain a degree of authority over how data derived from their biological and cultural resources is stored, interpreted, and disseminated. Malaysian law does not yet formally recognise a statutory right of collective data ownership. Nevertheless, instruments such as the Malaysian Code of Responsible Conduct in Research (MCRCR) frame data stewardship as an institutional responsibility grounded in transparency, accountability, and social responsibility (Council, 2020).

When applied to genomic repositories, this expectation suggests that ethical governance extends beyond obtaining initial consent to include ongoing consultation, benefit-sharing considerations, and culturally responsive communication. The absence of follow-up dialogue in this case reveals a governance gap between procedural compliance and relational legitimacy.

(D) TRUST, HISTORICAL CONTEXT, AND ETHICAL LEGITIMACY

For many Orang Asli communities, historical experiences of extractive research without reciprocal benefit contribute to heightened sensitivity regarding external data use. Even where confidentiality measures are technically adequate, failure to address communal expectations of feedback, recognition, or benefit sharing may erode trust. Ethical legitimacy in such contexts depends on demonstrable respect and transparency, rather than strict adherence to documentation procedures alone.

International normative frameworks reinforce this relational perspective. The OECD Guidelines on Human Biobanks and Genetic Research Databases emphasise custodianship, accountability, and transparency in long-term data governance, while CIOMS guidance highlights the need to consider social and group-based harms alongside individual privacy (CIOMS, 2016). These instruments collectively signal that sustainable Indigenous biobanking practices require equitable governance relationships rather than unilateral technical compliance.

Key Takeaways

- **Anonymisation is insufficient where metadata enables cultural or group identification.**
  Ethnic, linguistic, and geographic descriptors can function as indirect identifiers, engaging both technical security duties and ethical concerns regarding group harm.
- **Post-consent governance requires ongoing engagement, not one-time approval.**
  Secondary storage, cross-border processing, and benefit-sharing considerations should be communicated transparently and revisited where community interests are implicated.
- **Malaysia's framework recognises stewardship responsibilities but lacks explicit data sovereignty provisions.**
  Ministerial guidelines and professional codes encourage culturally responsive practices, yet statutory recognition of collective data rights remains limited.
- **Trust and reciprocity are integral to confidentiality governance in Indigenous contexts.**
  Feedback mechanisms, shared benefits, and transparent communication strengthen long-term participation and ethical legitimacy.
- **Failure to recognise collective privacy norms risks ethical harm and community disengagement.**
  Sustainable biobanking requires cultural humility, relational transparency, and governance models that acknowledge communal identity alongside individual data protection.

3.5 Concluding Reflections

This chapter has demonstrated that privacy and confidentiality in biobanking are not discrete procedural checkpoints but continuous governance obligations that persist long after initial consent has been obtained. Unlike traditional clinical encounters where data usage is temporally limited and purpose-specific, biobanks operate across extended timelines, evolving research objectives, and cross-jurisdictional collaborations. The ethical challenge therefore lies not merely in obtaining permission to collect biological materials, but in sustaining institutional stewardship over information whose meaning, sensitivity, and identifiability may transform over time.

Across the case studies, a consistent pattern emerges: confidentiality risks rarely arise from deliberate misconduct. More frequently, they stem from structural and systemic vulnerabilities, such as residual identifiers overlooked during data transfer, technological advances that outpace anonymisation techniques, secondary research uses that diverge from participant expectations, or metadata classifications that render entire communities identifiable. These scenarios illustrate that privacy protection in biobanking cannot be reduced to technical anonymisation or contractual assurances alone. Instead, it requires iterative verification, contextual awareness, and anticipatory governance capable of responding to both technological and social change.

A second recurring theme is the relational dimension of privacy. Genetic and health data are inherently interconnected; they implicate not only individual participants but also families, lineages, and communities. The Malaysian regulatory framework, particularly the Personal Data Protection Act 2010 and its amendments, provides a robust individual-centric baseline for data security and accountability. Yet the case analyses reveal that ethical adequacy often extends beyond statutory compliance. Familial reputation, cultural symbolism, posthumous dignity, and Indigenous collective identity introduce layers of concern that legal instruments do not always explicitly articulate but that ethics committees and research institutions must nonetheless navigate. Privacy, in this context, becomes a question of social legitimacy as much as legal permissibility.

The chapter also highlights the importance of transparency and communication as preventive safeguards. Several of the tensions examined did not arise from actual disclosure but from uncertainty, misunderstanding, or perceived loss of informational control. Cross-border data sharing, commercial partnerships, and secondary research trajectories can generate anxiety even where confidentiality protections remain intact. This underscores that ethical biobanking governance must address not only data security but also participant reassurance and clarity of expectations. Plain-language explanations, culturally responsive engagement, and periodic reaffirmation of data-handling practices function as integral components of confidentiality protection rather than supplementary gestures.

From an institutional perspective, privacy and confidentiality emerge as indicators of governance integrity. Breaches or misalignments erode public trust, diminish research participation, and compromise the sustainability of national biobank initiatives. Conversely, demonstrable accountability, through audit mechanisms, layered access controls, breach-response transparency, and ethics-committee oversight, reinforces confidence and strengthens collaborative networks. The emphasis therefore shifts from reactive compliance toward a privacy-by-design paradigm, embedding safeguards within infrastructural and procedural architecture rather than treating them as post-incident corrections.

Finally, the Malaysian context illustrates both the strengths and evolving frontiers of biobank governance. Existing legislation, ministerial guidelines, and international ethical frameworks collectively establish a substantive normative foundation for confidentiality protection. Yet emerging issues such as digital re-identification, posthumous sample use, and collective data sovereignty signal areas where ethical reflection must continue to develop alongside scientific advancement. The task for policymakers and institutions is not merely to close regulatory gaps, but to cultivate a governance culture that recognises privacy and confidentiality as dynamic ethical commitments grounded in respect, accountability, and relational trust.

In summary, privacy in biobanking is neither static nor purely technical. It is a sustained practice of stewardship that balances scientific progress with human dignity, individual rights with communal identity, and legal compliance with cultural legitimacy. Where these elements are integrated, biobanks can function not only as repositories of biological data but also as trusted custodians of personal and collective narratives that underpin responsible biomedical innovation.

References

Human Tissue Act. (1974).

International Ethical Guidelines for Health-Related Research Involving Humans. (2016). CIOMS.

The Working Committee for the Establishment of the National Biorepository Policy for Malaysia. (2023). A Tecnical Report: The Roadmap to Establishing the National Biorepository Policy for Malaysia. National Laboratory Technical Advisory Committee (LTAC). Retrieved January 12, 2026, from https://mkak.moh.gov.my/index.php/muat-turun/penerbitan?download=33:technical-report-concept-note-biorepositories-p-g-edited-22-aug-2023

Malaysian Code of Responsible Conduct in Research. (2020).

Malaysian Guideline for Good Clinical Practice. (2018). Health.

Malaysian Guidelines on the Use of Human Biological Samples for Research. (2025). Malaysia Ministry of Health.

OECD Guidelines and Human Biobanks and Genetic Research Databases. (2009). OECD.

Personal Data Protection (Amendment) Act. (2024).

Personal Data Protection Act. (2010).

Pullman, D., Etchegary, H., Gallagher, K., Hodgkinson, K., Keough, M., Morgan, D., & Street, C. (2012). Personal privacy, public benefits, and biobanks: A conjoint analysis of policy priorities and public perceptions. *Genetics in Medicine*, *14*(2), 229–235. https://doi.org/10.1038/gim.0b013e31822e578f

Siminoff, L. A., Wilson-Genderson, M., Mosavel, M., Barker, L., Trgina, J., & Traino, H. M. (2017). Confidentiality in biobanking research: A comparison of donor and nondonor families' understanding of risks. *Genetic Testing and Molecular Biomarkers*, *21*(3), 171–177. https://doi.org/10.1089/gtmb.2016.0407

Takai-Igarashi, T., Kinoshita, K., Nagasaki, M., Ogishima, S., Nakamura, N., Nagase, S., Nagaie, S., Saito, T., Nagami, F., Minegishi, N., Suzuki, Y., Suzuki, K., Hashizume, H., Kuriyama, S., Hozawa, A., Yaegashi, N., Kure,

S., Tamiya, G., Kawaguchi, Y.,. . . Yamamoto, M. (2017). Security controls in an integrated biobank to protect privacy in data sharing: Rationale and study design. *BMC Medical Informatics and Decision Making*, *17*(1), 100. https://doi.org/10.1186/s12911-017-0494-5

Universal Declaration on Bioethics and Human Rights. (2006). UNESCO.

4 The Commercialisation of Biobanks

4.1 Introduction: Commercialisation and the Transformation of Biobank Governance

Biobanks were initially conceived as public-interest research infrastructures, grounded in the language of altruism, solidarity, and collective scientific advancement. Participants were typically invited to contribute biological materials under the assurance that their donation would advance medical knowledge and generate long-term societal benefit. Over time, however, the operational realities of maintaining large-scale repositories, such as high storage costs, data-processing expenses, and the increasing value of genomic analytics, have drawn biobanks into closer engagement with private-sector actors. Pharmaceutical companies, biotechnology firms, data-analytics enterprises, and intellectual-property regimes now form part of the contemporary biobank ecosystem.

Commercialisation in this context does not refer solely to profit generation. Rather, it encompasses a continuum of market-adjacent practices – licensing agreements, fee-for-access models, public–private partnerships, patenting of downstream innovations, and exclusive collaboration contracts. These mechanisms may enhance research efficiency and financial sustainability, yet they simultaneously recalibrate the moral and relational narrative of donation. Biological materials originally framed as contributions to a collective scientific endeavour risk being reinterpreted as inputs into proprietary value chains, thereby shifting the ethical meaning of participation from solidarity toward instrumental value (Garden et al., 2021).

The ethical concern, therefore, is not whether commercial participation should be categorically excluded, but whether the conditions, transparency, and distributive consequences of such participation remain consistent with the expectations under which donations were made. The "charitable trust" governance model, for instance, emphasises fiduciary duties and beneficiary interests rather than ownership claims, highlighting that the legitimacy of commercial engagement depends less on the presence of profit and more on the integrity of stewardship structures (Boggio, 2005). Parallel policy discourse similarly stresses that commercialisation is ethically contingent rather than inherently

DOI: 10.4324/9781003745785-4

problematic, provided that governance mechanisms preserve accountability, public value, and participatory legitimacy (Garden et al., 2021).

4.2 Conceptual Foundations of Commercialisation

4.2.1 Commodification and the Moral Meaning of Donation

Commercialisation introduces the risk that human biological materials, originally donated under altruistic premises, may be perceived as commodities. This transformation alters the symbolic meaning of participation. Donation framed as solidarity or intergenerational contribution may be retrospectively interpreted as unpaid labour contributing to private profit, particularly where downstream benefits are asymmetrically distributed. Contemporary analyses of organoid and precision-medicine research demonstrate that commercial framing can undermine inclusivity and willingness to donate, especially among historically marginalised communities (van Daal & Jongsma, 2025).

The ethical tension therefore lies not in financial sustainability itself but in moral asymmetry, where donors contribute without expectation of profit while private actors accumulate economic value. Such asymmetry raises concerns regarding dignity, fairness, and the redefinition of biological materials as tradable assets detached from the donor's original moral intent (McMahon & Kolawole, 2024).

4.2.2 Intellectual Property and Downstream Access

Intellectual property regimes further complicate the ethical landscape. Donors often consent under the expectation of public benefit, yet therapeutic or diagnostic technologies derived from their biological materials may become patented, restricting affordability or accessibility. This creates a structural divergence between publicly sourced inputs and privately controlled outputs.

Scholarly examinations of IP governance in biobanking highlight the absence of binding disclosure obligations requiring institutions to inform donors of how intellectual-property rights may influence downstream access to health technologies (McMahon & Kolawole, 2024). From a bioethical standpoint, this gap affects both autonomy, through insufficient informational transparency, and justice, where exclusivity mechanisms may undermine the distributive rationale that justified initial participation.

4.2.3 Public Trust and the "Commercialisation Effect"

Empirical literature consistently demonstrates what has been termed the "commercialisation effect" – a measurable decline in public trust and willingness to donate where commercial involvement is perceived as opaque or inequitable

(Walshe et al., 2024). Trust in biobanking is not merely reputational; it functions as a structural precondition for participation and dataset diversity. Importantly, these studies indicate that public discomfort arises less from the presence of commercial actors than from opacity, unequal benefit distribution, and perceived loss of control. Commercialisation therefore becomes ethically problematic when governance practices fail to preserve transparency and reciprocity rather than when profit itself is present (Samuel, Hardcastle, et al., 2022).

4.3 Regulatory and Policy Landscape in Malaysia

Malaysia does not possess a single statute dedicated exclusively to the commercialisation of biobanks. Governance instead emerges through an interlocking framework of data-protection legislation, research-ethics guidelines, contractual law, and ministerial instruments regulating the handling and transfer of biological materials. Commercialisation therefore operates within distributed regulatory oversight rather than a unified legal regime, requiring institutions to navigate overlapping statutory and ethical duties.

4.3.1 Personal Data Protection Act 2010 (PDPA)

Where commercial activities involve identifiable or pseudonymised participant data, the Personal Data Protection Act 2010 becomes directly applicable. Several provisions are particularly relevant in commercial biobank partnerships ("Personal Data Protection Act", 2010).

Section 6 – General Principle

Requires personal data to be processed with consent and for lawful purposes. In commercial contexts, this provision implicitly limits expansion of data use beyond purposes originally communicated to participants.

Section 7 – Notice and Choice Principle

Obliges data users to inform data subjects of processing purposes and the class of third parties to whom data may be disclosed. Commercial access arrangements fall squarely within "material information" affecting participant expectations.

Section 8 – Disclosure Principle

Restricts disclosure of personal data without consent except under lawful authority. Commercial sharing arrangements must therefore align with previously notified purposes or obtain renewed authorisation.

Section 9 – Security Principle

Mandates "practical steps" to protect personal data from misuse or unauthorised access. In commercial collaborations, this extends beyond technical safeguards to include contractual confidentiality clauses, audit mechanisms, and role-based access controls.

Section 129 – Cross-Border Transfer

Regulates transfer of personal data outside Malaysia, requiring assurance that the receiving jurisdiction provides adequate protection or equivalent contractual safeguards. Multinational commercial data flows are directly implicated under this provision.

Collectively, these provisions impose continuing accountability obligations on biobanks even where profit-generating arrangements exist, reinforcing that commercial engagement does not extinguish fiduciary-like duties toward participants.

4.3.2 Ministry of Health Guidelines on the Use of Human Biological Samples

The Malaysian Guidelines on the Use of Human Biological Samples for Research provide sector-specific ethical direction relevant to commercial engagement (Malaysia Ministry of Health, 2025).

Key expectations include:

- Requirement for Material Transfer Agreements (MTAs) where samples are shared with third parties;
- Mandatory ethics-committee review for secondary or collaborative use;
- Emphasis on transparency and participant information regarding future use and potential partnerships.

Although not statutory law, these guidelines function as normative benchmarks within research institutions and are routinely relied upon by ethics committees in evaluating commercial proposals.

4.3.3 Malaysian Code of Responsible Conduct in Research (MCRCR)

The MCRCR reinforces institutional duties of integrity, accountability, and social responsibility (Council, 2020). In the context of commercialisation, it frames data and sample stewardship as an organisational obligation rather than as an individual researcher's discretion. The Code implicitly discourages extractive practices by emphasising responsible data management, transparency, and avoidance of conflicts of interest.

4.3.4 International Normative Instruments

Malaysia's governance landscape is further informed by international instruments, such as the OECD Guidelines on Human Biobanks and Genetic Research Databases, which emphasise benefit-sharing, transparency, and equitable access in commercial and cross-border collaborations (Garden et al., 2021). Although they are non-binding, these frameworks exert persuasive influence on domestic policy interpretation and ethics-committee reasoning, situating commercialisation within a broader discourse of innovation balanced with public good.

4.4 Case Studies

4.4.1 Case Study 1: Public-Private Partnership in a Malaysian Biobank

Case Narrative

The GenomeMalaysia Biobank was established within a public university hospital through government funding to collect DNA and tissue samples for health research. After several years of operation, the biobank entered into a partnership with BioPharm Sdn Bhd, a private pharmaceutical company. Under the agreement, BioPharm provided financial investment, sequencing technology, and bioinformatics infrastructure in exchange for privileged access to selected rare-disease samples and associated datasets. The collaboration aimed to accelerate the development of diagnostic tools and therapeutics, potentially resulting in commercially valuable patents.

Biobank leadership presented the partnership as a sustainability strategy and a pathway to translational impact. However, unease emerged among participants and researchers. Some donors questioned whether their contributions to a publicly funded repository were now being redirected toward private profit without adequate disclosure. Academic researchers expressed concern that BioPharm's commercial priorities might influence research direction. Tensions intensified when BioPharm proposed temporary exclusivity over certain datasets, limiting access by external academic teams. In response, the biobank's ethics advisory panel convened to evaluate whether the partnership complied with Malaysian legal and ethical standards and whether it preserved the institution's public-interest mandate.

Commentary

This scenario illustrates a central dilemma in contemporary biobanking governance, that is, the convergence of public stewardship and private capital. Public-private partnerships (PPPs) are not inherently unethical. On the one hand, they may provide financial sustainability, technical capacity, and accelerated pathways to innovation. On the other hand, ethical legitimacy depends on whether such partnerships preserve the relational and fiduciary expectations under which biological materials were originally donated.

Scholarly analyses consistently warn that commercial involvement, if poorly disclosed or inadequately governed, may recalibrate the moral narrative of donation from solidarity toward instrumental extraction (Garden et al., 2021). The ethical tension here does not lie in profit generation per se, but in informational asymmetry and value concentration, particularly where donors perceive that privately captured benefits diverge from publicly stated purposes.

(A)CONSENT ADEQUACY AND DISCLOSURE OF COMMERCIAL INTENT

A recurring governance concern is whether initial consent processes adequately addressed the possibility of commercial use. Malaysian ministerial guidance, particularly the Malaysian Guidelines on the Use of Human Biological Samples for Research, emphasises that participant information sheets should disclose potential secondary uses, including collaborations with private entities (Malaysia Ministry of Health, 2025). Where such disclosure is absent or vague, ethical duties of re-notification or renewed consent may arise, not because the partnership is unlawful but because donor expectations may have been formed under incomplete information.

Empirical research examining participant communication practices shows that commercial access is often mentioned abstractly without clarifying exclusivity clauses, patent implications, or benefit distribution, thereby producing procedurally valid but substantively thin consent (Samuel, Hardcastle, et al., 2022).

(B)DATA GOVERNANCE AND STATUTORY COMPLIANCE

The involvement of a private entity introduces direct applicability of the "Personal Data Protection Act" (2010). Several provisions are particularly salient:

- **Section 7 – Notice and Choice Principle**: requires disclosure of the class of third parties receiving data. A commercial collaborator constitutes material information affecting participant expectations.
- **Section 8 – Disclosure Principle**: restricts onward disclosure beyond notified purposes.
- **Section 9 – Security Principle**: mandates practical safeguards, including contractual confidentiality obligations and audit mechanisms.
- **Section 129 – Cross-Border Transfer**: regulates multinational data flows where foreign processing occurs.

Notably, while public universities may enjoy partial statutory exemptions in certain contexts, the moment when data enters a commercial processing environment, the regulatory threshold shifts toward full PDPA applicability. Thus,

PPP agreements must incorporate explicit compliance clauses to avoid legal and reputational risk.

(C)INTELLECTUAL PROPERTY AND BENEFIT-SHARING

The prospect of patents arising from publicly donated samples introduces questions of distributive justice. Malaysian patent law permits proprietary claims over downstream innovations; however, no statutory provision mandates donor profit-sharing. The ethical issue is, therefore, not legal entitlement but equitable reciprocity.

Recent bioethical analyses underscore that intellectual-property regimes may unintentionally sever the moral link between donation and public benefit, particularly when exclusive licensing restricts affordability or accessibility (McMahon & Kolawole, 2024). International guidance, including OECD biobank frameworks, encourages the articulation of benefit-sharing policies, ranging from reinvestment into public health infrastructure to conditional licensing clauses ensuring affordable access (OECD, 2009).

In PPP contexts, exclusivity arrangements, such as temporary dataset monopolies, are especially sensitive. Although not unlawful, they may undermine the open-science ethos traditionally associated with publicly funded repositories and intensify perceptions of commodification.

(D)TRANSPARENCY, TRUST, AND INSTITUTIONAL LEGITIMACY

Empirical literature on the "commercialisation effect" demonstrates that public trust declines when commercial involvement is perceived as opaque or extractive (Walshe et al., 2024). In this scenario, stakeholder discomfort arises less from the existence of BioPharm's involvement than from uncertainty regarding exclusivity, profit allocation, and governance oversight. Transparency therefore functions not merely as a communication strategy but as a preventive ethical safeguard.

Professional and ethical codes in Malaysia, including the Malaysian Code of Responsible Conduct in Research (MCRCR), frame stewardship as an institutional duty grounded in accountability, conflict-of-interest management, and social responsibility (Council, 2020). The challenge is to ensure that commercial partnerships do not displace the biobank's identity as a public-interest custodian.

Key Takeaways

- **Commercial partnerships are ethically contingent, not inherently problematic.**
  Legitimacy depends on transparency, reciprocity, and preservation of public-interest stewardship.

- **Consent processes must explicitly address potential commercial use and exclusivity clauses.**
  Procedural consent without substantive disclosure risks informational asymmetry and erosion of trust.
- **PDPA obligations intensify once private entities process participant data.**
  Sections 7, 8, 9, and 129 collectively impose disclosure, security, and cross-border accountability duties.
- **Intellectual-property outcomes require ethical benefit-sharing considerations even where not legally mandated.**
  Conditional licensing, reinvestment, or community health benefits can mitigate perceptions of commodification.
- **Exclusivity arrangements may undermine open-science norms and public legitimacy.**
  Time-limited or narrowly scoped exclusivity clauses should be justified and transparently communicated.
- **Institutional stewardship is the core governance principle.**
  Professional codes such as the MCRCR emphasise accountability, conflict-of-interest management, and transparency as safeguards against extractive commercial practices.

4.4.2 Case Study 2: Cross-Border Collaboration and Biospecimen Export

Case Narrative

A Malaysian cancer biobank based at a university research hospital joined an international consortium investigating genetic markers for rare cancers. The project was co-funded by a foreign pharmaceutical sponsor and a Malaysian government grant, requiring the export of approximately 500 tumour and blood specimen sets to a specialised genomics laboratory in Europe.

While the scientific rationale was clear, governance complications emerged during implementation. The original donor consent documentation did not expressly mention overseas transfer or potential commercial collaboration. Several contributors originated from rural and Indigenous communities, heightening cultural and ethical sensitivity regarding foreign handling of biological materials. Concurrently, the research team had not secured the necessary export permits nor finalised a Material Transfer Agreement (MTA).

Negotiations over the MTA proved contentious. The foreign sponsor sought flexibility to conduct additional analyses and retain leftover specimens for future proprietary research, whereas the Malaysian Institutional Review Board (IRB) insisted that samples be used solely for the approved study and that remaining materials be destroyed or repatriated. Shipment was temporarily suspended pending confirmation that the collaboration satisfied domestic regulatory and ethical standards.

Commentary

This scenario illustrates how cross-border biospecimen export transforms research collaboration into a transaction involving both scientific data and potential commercial value. The movement of biological materials beyond national jurisdiction is not merely logistical, but it also implicates issues of custodianship, downstream intellectual property, and long-term control over biological resources.

(D)STEWARDSHIP, OWNERSHIP, AND MATERIAL TRANSFER AGREEMENTS

At the centre of the dispute lies the distinction between stewardship and ownership. Malaysian regulatory and ethical instruments consistently frame biobanks as custodians rather than as proprietors of donated samples. An MTA therefore functions not only as a contractual safeguard but as a commercial governance mechanism that defines permissible use, restricts derivative exploitation, and preserves the originating institution's supervisory authority.

International policy discourse, including OECD biobank governance frameworks, emphasises that MTAs should articulate limits on secondary commercial use, conditions for intellectual-property claims, and obligations for sample return or destruction (Garden et al., 2021). Where foreign collaborators request indefinite retention of specimens, the risk shifts from collaborative research toward resource extraction and proprietary accumulation.

(B)CONSENT AND CROSS-BORDER VALUE TRANSFER

Although consent is often discussed in privacy terms, in cross-border commercial collaborations it also functions as authorisation for value transfer. If donors were not informed that their biological materials might leave the country or be used in profit-oriented contexts, the ethical issue extends beyond autonomy into misalignment of economic expectations.

Empirical analyses of participant communication practices indicate that commercial implications of international data or specimen sharing are frequently under-explained, producing consent that is procedurally valid yet economically opaque (Samuel, Hardcastle, et al., 2022). In such cases, ethics committees may require renewed notification or conditional approval rather than outright prohibition.

(C)STATUTORY AND REGULATORY OBLIGATIONS

The "Personal Data Protection Act" (2010) becomes engaged where identifiable or linked data accompany exported specimens. In particular:

- **Section 7 – Notice and Choice Principle** requires disclosure of foreign recipients;
- **Section 8 – Disclosure Principle** restricts onward use beyond approved purposes;
- **Section 129 – Cross-Border Transfer** requires assurance of equivalent protection or explicit consent.

Beyond data protection, Malaysian administrative mechanisms such as export permits through the BLESS system enforce biosafety, traceability, and legal accountability. These regulatory layers collectively affirm that cross-border biospecimen movement is subject to dual oversight: ethical and commercial-regulatory.

(D)INTELLECTUAL PROPERTY AND DOWNSTREAM COMMERCIAL CONTROL

The foreign sponsor's request to retain leftover samples reflects a broader concern regarding future proprietary claims. Retention of physical specimens facilitates additional analyses that may yield patentable discoveries without further involvement of the source institution. Scholarly critiques note that such arrangements risk severing the moral link between donor contribution and public benefit, particularly when exclusive licensing restricts access to resulting diagnostics or therapies (McMahon & Kolawole, 2024).

Ethically, the issue is not the generation of intellectual property itself but rather the absence of reciprocal mechanisms – whether through joint authorship, co-ownership of patents, technology transfer, or affordable access clauses.

(E)BENEFIT-SHARING AND EQUITABLE COLLABORATION

International ethical frameworks, including CIOMS (2016) and OECD (2009) guidance, consistently emphasise benefit-sharing in cross-border research partnerships. Benefit-sharing need not imply direct financial compensation; it may include capacity-building, training of local researchers, infrastructure investment, or preferential licensing of resulting technologies. Empirical literature on the "commercialisation effect" demonstrates that public trust declines where collaborations appear extractive or one-sided (Walshe et al., 2024). In this context, equitable negotiation of MTAs and transparency regarding future use function as preventive governance tools, reinforcing the perception that international collaboration remains a partnership rather than a transfer of biological assets.

Key Takeaways

- **Biospecimen export is a transfer of both scientific and commercial value.**
  Governance mechanisms must address downstream ownership, not merely logistical handling.
- **Material Transfer Agreements are core commercial-governance instruments.**
  They should define permissible use, IP implications, and conditions for destruction or return of unused samples.
- **Consent in cross-border contexts authorises value transfer as well as data use.**
  Incomplete disclosure of international commercial implications risks ethical misalignment.
- **PDPA Sections 7, 8, and 129 impose disclosure and cross-border accountability duties.**
  Export accompanied by identifiable data triggers statutory obligations.
- **Indefinite foreign retention of specimens heightens proprietary risk.**
  It may facilitate unilateral patent claims and weaken the originating institution's stewardship role.
- **Benefit-sharing and capacity-building sustain legitimacy.**
  Equitable collaboration mitigates the "commercialisation effect" and reinforces public trust.

4.4.3 Case Study 3: Commercialisation Involving Indigenous Communities in Malaysia

Case Narrative

The **Orang Asli Health Genome Initiative** is a hypothetical genomics project led by a Malaysian public university and an international biotech start-up. The initiative aims to study genetic variants among an Orang Asli community in Peninsular Malaysia to better understand disease resistance and identify potential therapeutic targets.

Before recruitment, the research team conducted several community briefings with community leaders and a village committee. Individual blood samples were collected after participants signed consent forms in Bahasa Malaysia. The briefings emphasised potential *public health* benefits, such as better screening, future treatments, and improved understanding of community health risks. The consent materials included a general statement that "research findings may lead to new products", but the project was consistently framed in community meetings as a **health-focused, educational collaboration**.

Two years later, researchers identified a **novel genetic variant** with potential relevance for glucose metabolism. The biotech partner filed a **patent**

application covering the use of the variant in developing an anti-diabetic therapeutic pathway and began discussions with larger pharmaceutical firms. The community learned of the patent filing through media reporting and advocacy networks, generating intense backlash. Community members described the situation as "outsiders profiting from Orang Asli blood", and elders expressed concern that the community's contribution was being converted into private property without meaningful reciprocity.

The university's ethics governance team was forced into crisis management: the community demanded an explanation, asked what the patent means, and requested assurances that (i) no further commercial steps would be taken without their involvement, and (ii) the community would share in any benefits if a product was developed.

Commentary

(A) CONSENT VALIDITY WHEN COMMERCIALISATION BECOMES CONCRETE

This case is not primarily about whether consent forms mentioned commercial use but whether participants understood the **practical implications of commercialisation**, especially patent claims and downstream product development. International guidance on biobanking consent treats commercial use as "material information" that should be disclosed clearly, including whether commercial products may be developed and whether participants will receive any monetary or other benefits (CIOMS, 2016, Guidelines 11 and 12). A critical point is that "possible commercialisation" is not ethically equivalent to "we may file patents over discoveries derived from your samples." The dissonance between donor expectations (public benefit/altruism) and downstream IP practices has been identified as a structural ethical risk in biobanking (McMahon & Kolawole, 2024).

Within the Malaysian context, this expectation is reinforced by the Malaysian Guidelines on the Use of Human Biological Samples for Research (2nd ed.), which require disclosure of secondary and commercial uses and emphasise that consent must be meaningful rather than perfunctory, particularly where long-term storage or third-party access is anticipated. The ethical problem therefore is not solved by a generic clause; it requires comprehension, culturally appropriate explanation, and governance safeguards that remain credible once commercial value emerges.

(B) BENEFIT-SHARING IS NOT OPTIONAL IN POPULATION-LEVEL STUDIES INVOLVING VULNERABLE GROUPS

This case should be clearly distinguished from Case 1 and Case 2 – the core tension is who benefits when a community-linked genetic variant becomes commercially valuable.

The OECD Guidelines on Human Biobanks and Genetic Research Databases (2009) place benefit-sharing and commercialisation policies at the centre of custodianship (OECD, 2009). They recommend:

- a *benefit-sharing policy* addressing whether products/tests will be shared with the community and how (Best Practices 9.1), and
- negotiating benefit-sharing agreements before studies begin, especially in population-level studies involving vulnerable populations or unique concerns (Best Practices 9.2)

Although Malaysia does not impose statutory profit-sharing duties, the Malaysian Code of Responsible Conduct in Research (MCRCR) frames stewardship in terms of fairness, accountability, and avoidance of exploitative research relationships. When read alongside OECD guidance, this creates a soft-law expectation of reciprocity, particularly where communities contribute distinctive biological or cultural resources.

In this case, the absence of a clear, negotiated benefit-sharing framework makes the patent filing appear extractive even if it is technically lawful. The governance failure is **ex ante** because there is no concrete agreement existed on what "public benefit" would mean once intellectual property became relevant.

3. COMMERCIALISATION GOVERNANCE AND TRANSPARENCY DUTIES

OECD guidance through its Principle 9C further expects biobanks to have and communicate explicit policies on commercialisation and intellectual-property management, including clarification of rights retained over samples and data. This matters because patenting can be experienced socially as asserting ownership over community-derived biological knowledge, even though, legally, patents concern applications and inventions rather than ownership of persons or DNA.

In Malaysia, comparable transparency duties can be inferred from:

- the Malaysian Guidelines on the Use of Human Biological Samples for Research, which emphasise disclosure of third-party access and custodianship responsibilities; and
- the Personal Data Protection Act 2010, particularly the Notice and Choice Principle (Section 7) and Disclosure Principle (Section 8), which require organisations to inform data subjects of the purpose and class of third parties receiving personal data.

A practical governance mechanism to prevent "commercialisation shocks" is a participant- and community-communication model that explicitly frames:

- who may access the resource (including commercial actors),
- how benefits are framed, and

- what participants will not receive (e.g., direct financial returns where that is institutional policy).

A scholarly work shows that biobanks increasingly manage these expectations through participant-facing materials and layered consent explanations rather than by relying solely on legal disclaimers (Samuel, Hardcastle, et al., 2022).

4. HEIGHTENED ETHICAL SENSITIVITY FOR INDIGENOUS POPULATIONS

This case also sits within a broader ethical backdrop whereby international bioethics instruments explicitly recognise that unethical scientific conduct has disproportionately affected Indigenous and local communities and that such communities possess special needs requiring protection and fairness (UNESCO, 2006, Articles 8 and 12).

Malaysia does not currently have a dedicated statute governing Indigenous genetic resources; however, domestic research-ethics guidance consistently emphasises respect, non-exploitation, and culturally responsive engagement when working with marginalised populations. The MCRCR and ministerial research guidelines implicitly recognise that formal legal sufficiency does not exhaust ethical responsibility.

Accordingly, standard individualistic consent approaches may be insufficient where commercialisation affects collective identity, dignity, and community welfare. The ethical question becomes whether the community is treated merely as a biological resource pool or as a partner in governance and benefit determination.

5. ETHICS REVIEW RESPONSIBILITIES WHEN THE PROJECT CHANGES DIRECTION

Once the project moved from discovery to patent filing and commercial negotiations, that shift should trigger renewed ethics-governance scrutiny, not because patenting is inherently impermissible, but because it materially alters the participant risk-benefit landscape and the meaning of consent. International guidance expects ethics review structures to remain active in assessing social and legal implications of research transitions (UNESCO, 2006, Articles 19 and 20)

In the Malaysian setting, although no statute expressly mandates re-approval for intellectual-property actions, institutional review boards commonly interpret major commercial developments as ethically significant deviations requiring reassessment. This interpretation aligns with the MCRCR's accountability and integrity principles, which expect researchers to remain responsive to participant welfare and community expectations throughout the research lifecycle.

At a minimum, good governance would require:

(i) disclosure to the ethics committee of the IP intention,
(ii) assessment of consistency with the original consent narrative and community expectations, and
(iii) a concrete plan for benefit-sharing and community engagement before commercial steps proceed.

Key Takeaways

- **Commercialisation must be intelligible, not merely mentioned.**
  Consent processes should clearly explain patenting and downstream product development in culturally appropriate terms. Generic "future research" clauses are insufficient, particularly in light of expectations under the *Malaysian Guidelines on the Use of Human Biological Samples for Research* and CIOMS consent standards.
- **Benefit-sharing is a governance expectation in community-linked research.**
  Even where Malaysian law does not mandate profit distribution, OECD guidance and the *Malaysian Code of Responsible Conduct in Research (MCRCR)* frame reciprocity and fairness as core stewardship duties. Absence of prior benefit-sharing arrangements risks perceptions of biopiracy or extraction.
- **Commercialisation policies must be transparent from the outset.**
  Biobanks should communicate who may access samples, the possibility of intellectual-property claims, and the limits of participant entitlements. This aligns with OECD best practices and the transparency principles reflected in PDPA 2010 under its Sections 7 (Notice and Choice Principles) and 8 (Disclosure Principle).
- **Indigenous contexts require collective as well as individual ethical consideration.**
  Where research implicates communal identity or cultural dignity, reliance on purely individual consent may be inadequate. Malaysian ethical guidance and international bioethics instruments recognise heightened duties of respect and non-exploitation toward vulnerable communities.
- **Ethics oversight must continue when projects shift toward IP or licensing.**
  Patent filings and commercial negotiations represent material governance transitions. Institutional review boards and research-integrity frameworks such as the *MCRCR* should reassess consistency with original consent narratives and community welfare.

4.4.4 Case Study 4: Monetisation, Cost-Recovery, and the Biobank as a Data Marketplace

Case Narrative

The National Clinical Genomics Repository (NCGR), a university-affiliated Malaysian biobank established through a combination of Ministry of Health grants and research funding, had operated for nearly a decade primarily as a non-profit research infrastructure. Access to biospecimens and associated datasets was historically provided to local academic researchers at minimal administrative cost.

Facing declining public funding and rising operational expenses for data storage, sequencing maintenance, cybersecurity infrastructure, and personnel, the NCGR management introduced a tiered access and licensing model. Under the new structure:

- Malaysian public universities paid nominal fees;
- foreign academic institutions paid higher administrative charges; and
- pharmaceutical and biotechnology companies were required to purchase premium data-access licences and annual subscription packages.

The policy was framed internally as "cost-recovery and sustainability." However, controversy emerged when a group of long-time research participants learned that their anonymised genomic datasets were being licensed to commercial entities. Several donors argued that their participation had been motivated by altruism and the belief that their contributions would serve purely public research interests.

A civil-society organisation questioned whether the repository had effectively transformed into a data marketplace, arguing that charging premium licensing fees blurred the distinction between institutional sustainability and commodification of biological resources. The repository's governance board defended the policy, asserting that no physical samples were sold and that revenue was reinvested into research infrastructure. Nonetheless, the incident triggered public debate over whether monetising access to donated biological data, rather than the data itself, constituted an ethical boundary crossing.

Commentary

(A) COST-RECOVERY VS COMMODIFICATION: WHEN SUSTAINABILITY RESEMBLES PROFIT

Unlike patent-driven commercialisation, this case concerns institutional monetisation without ownership transfer. The ethical ambiguity arises because donors rarely distinguish between selling samples and selling *access* to the informational value derived from them.

Empirical literature on the "commercialisation effect" demonstrates that public willingness to participate declines when biobanks are perceived as revenue-generating enterprises, even if funds are reinvested into research infrastructure. The tension is therefore not purely economic but symbolic, whereby donors often view their contribution as a civic act rather than an asset entering a market exchange.

Within the Malaysian regulatory context, no statute expressly prohibits cost-recovery mechanisms. However, the Malaysian Guidelines on the Use of Human Biological Samples for Research emphasise custodianship and public-interest orientation, implicitly cautioning against framing human biological materials as tradable commodities. The ethical question becomes whether tiered pricing constitutes reasonable sustainability or a subtle shift toward commercial asset logic.

(B) TRANSPARENCY AND EXPECTATION ALIGNMENT UNDER DATA PROTECTION PRINCIPLES

Even when data is anonymised, transparency regarding access and licensing practices remains crucial. The Personal Data Protection Act 2010, while primarily focused on identifiable personal data, embeds broader transparency norms through the Notice and Choice Principle (Section 7) and Disclosure Principle (Section 8). These provisions require organisations to inform data subjects of the purpose and class of third parties involved in data processing.

Although anonymised datasets may fall outside strict statutory obligations, applying PDPA-style transparency standards serves as a governance safeguard. Donors who discover monetisation retrospectively often experience a sense of **expectational betrayal**, not legal harm. It can be argued that if a biobank employed communication practices that explicitly disclosing the possibility of commercial access during recruitment, this would significantly mitigate later distrust.

(C) INSTITUTIONAL STEWARDSHIP AND FIDUCIARY RESPONSIBILITY

This case introduces a dimension absent from earlier scenarios, whereby the biobank is a financial actor rather than a research collaborator. International governance literature increasingly characterises biobanks as operating under a fiduciary or public-trust model, where custodians are expected to manage resources for collective benefit rather than for institutional profit (Henderson et al., 2013; Samuel, Broekstra, et al., 2022).

The Malaysian Code of Responsible Conduct in Research (MCRCR) reinforces this orientation by emphasising integrity, accountability, and avoidance of exploitative relationships. Although the Code does not forbid revenue generation, it frames research stewardship as involving proportionality and fairness. Tiered access fees therefore demand justification in terms of cost-recovery transparency and reinvestment clarity, rather than revenue maximisation.

(D) THE BOUNDARY BETWEEN ACCESS LICENSING AND DATA BROKERAGE

A further ethical risk is mission drift, where cost-recovery evolves into competitive pricing, exclusive licensing, or data-brokerage practices. Once datasets are treated as premium assets, pressures may arise to prioritise commercially lucrative collaborations over public-interest research.

International policy discussions, including OECD biobank governance frameworks, caution that monetisation models must be accompanied by explicit commercialisation policies and independent oversight to prevent inequitable access or erosion of scientific openness. The ethical issue is, therefore, not the presence of fees but the absence of principled limits and review mechanisms.

(E) PARTICIPANT PERCEPTION AND THE MORAL ECONOMY OF DONATION

This case uniquely highlights the moral economy of biobanking – the shared understanding that participation is grounded in solidarity rather than transaction. Research on donor attitudes shows that participants are more accepting of commercial access when benefits are clearly framed as infrastructural sustainability rather than as profit extraction.

In the Malaysian context, where public universities and hospitals often carry implicit social-service identities, monetisation without narrative framing risks reputational damage even if it is legally permissible. The governance challenge is therefore communicative as much as financial because sustaining public trust requires continuous articulation of purpose, limits, and reinvestment pathways.

Key Takeaways

- **Cost-recovery is ethically distinguishable from profit-making, but only when transparently justified.**
  Donors interpret monetisation symbolically and, therefore, sustainability narratives must be explicit and credible.
- **Transparency duties extend beyond identifiable data.**
  Sections 7 and 8 of the PDPA 2010 establish disclosure norms that biobanks should emulate even for anonymised datasets.
- **Biobanks operate under stewardship, not ownership.**
  Instruments such as the *Malaysian Code of Responsible Conduct in Research (MCRCR)* frame revenue generation as acceptable only when aligned with fairness and accountability.
- **Access licensing must avoid mission drift into data brokerage.**
  Independent oversight and explicit commercialisation policies are essential to preserve scientific openness and public legitimacy.
- **Public trust depends on narrative alignment.**
  Participants are more accepting of commercial access when it is framed as infrastructure sustainability rather than as commodification of donation.

4.5 Concluding Reflections

This chapter has examined the commercialisation of biobanks not as an isolated ethical dilemma, but as a progressively intensifying governance challenge. Through four escalating case studies, it has shown how seemingly minor ethical compromises, particularly in relation to transparency, consent, and expectation alignment, can compound as biobanking activities expand across institutional forms, national borders, economic models, and social contexts.

At the foundational level, the profit-driven private or semi-private biobank illustrates how broad consent and strategic silence can enable the quiet conversion of altruistic donation into economic capital. Such practices may be legally defensible in the absence of dedicated biobank legislation, but they remain ethically fragile, relying more on informational asymmetry than on genuine participant comprehension. This fragility is not resolved, but rather obscured, when similar commercial practices are embedded within public institutions through public-private partnerships. In such settings, institutional legitimacy and public trust may inadvertently be mobilised to normalise exclusivity clauses, licensing control, and downstream inequities.

When commercialisation crosses borders, the ethical weaknesses identified at the domestic level become amplified. Cross-border data and biospecimen transfers introduce regulatory asymmetry, attenuate oversight, and further distance participants from decision-making processes that shape the use of their biological materials. De-identification, contractual compliance, and material transfer agreements, while necessary, often prove insufficient to address concerns of mission drift, benefit imbalance, and extractive research dynamics.

The involvement of Indigenous and marginalised communities marks a critical inflection point in commercial biobanking. Where research outputs intersect with collective identity, cultural dignity, and historical vulnerability, individual consent alone cannot meaningfully authorise downstream commercial use. In such contexts, commercialisation risks evolving into a form of cultural extraction, producing symbolic and material harms that procedural safeguards alone cannot fully mitigate. This scenario underscores the necessity of community-level governance, negotiated benefit-sharing, and shared authority over how research value is generated and represented, particularly in multicultural societies such as Malaysia.

The fourth case, focusing on monetisation and access-licensing models, reveals that commercialisation is not confined to patents or partnerships but also arises through institutional sustainability mechanisms. Tiered pricing, subscription access, and data-licensing arrangements blur the line between cost-recovery and commodification, challenging the moral economy of donation upon which many biobanks depend. Here, the ethical issue is not ownership of samples but the symbolic and relational implications of treating research infrastructures as market actors.

Taken together, these cases demonstrate that commercialisation is not merely a question of profit, but rather a test of how biobanks conceptualise their ethical obligations to participants and communities. Consent, while necessary, is insufficient as a standalone safeguard in commercially dynamic research environments. Ethical governance must therefore move beyond procedural compliance towards substantive principles of transparency, proportionality, reciprocity, stewardship, and accountability.

For Malaysia, these lessons point to the need for clearer and more coherent biobank-specific governance frameworks that address commercial use explicitly. Existing instruments, such as the Malaysian Guidelines on the Use of Human Biological Samples for Research, the Personal Data Protection Act 2010, and the Malaysian Code of Responsible Conduct in Research, provide important normative foundations, yet they operate in a fragmented and sector-specific manner. A more integrated framework could require meaningful disclosure of commercial intent, impose structured oversight over exclusivity and licensing arrangements, and embed benefit-sharing as a normative expectation rather than a discretionary gesture. Importantly, governance mechanisms must remain context-sensitive, recognising that research involving public institutions, cross-border collaborations, Indigenous communities, or monetisation models demands differentiated levels of ethical scrutiny.

This chapter also sets the stage for the next ethical frontier in biobanking – that is, the management of information generated through research. If Chapter 4 reveals the limits of consent in governing commercial value, Chapter 5 turns to another domain where consent proves equally insufficient – the return of incidental and secondary health findings. In both contexts, the underlying question remains constant – how should biobanks balance respect for autonomy with responsibility for the consequences of the knowledge they create?

In confronting these questions, biobanks are ultimately compelled to reckon with their dual identity – as engines of scientific progress and as custodians of human trust. How they navigate commercialisation will shape not only the legitimacy of biobanking practices but also the ethical character of biomedical research governance in Malaysia for years to come.

References

Boggio, A. (2005). Charitable trusts and human research genetic databases: The way forward? *Genomics, Society and Policy*, *1*(2), 41.

Garden, H., Hawkins, N., & Winickoff, D. (2021). Building and sustaining collaborative platforms in genomics and biobanks for health innovation (OECD Science, Technology and Industry Policy Papers). OECD.

Henderson, G. E., Edwards, T. P., Cadigan, R. J., Davis, A. M., Zimmer, C., Conlon, I., & Weiner, B. J. (2013). Stewardship practices of U.S. biobanks. *Science Translational Medicine*, *5*(215), 215cm217. https://doi.org/10.1126/scitranslmed.3007362

International Ethical Guidelines for Health-Related Research Involving Humans. (2016). CIOMS.

Malaysian Code of Responsible Conduct in Research. (2020).

Malaysian Guidelines on the Use of Human Biological Samples for Research. (2025). Malaysia Ministry of Health.

McMahon, A. M., & Kolawole, O. I. (2024). Biobank donation in search of public benefits and the potential impact of intellectual property rights over access to health-technologies developed: A focus on the bioethical implications. *Medical Law Review*, *32*(2), 205–228. https://doi.org/10.1093/medlaw/fwae010

OECD Guidelines and Human Biobanks and Genetic Research Databases. (2009). OECD.

Personal Data Protection Act. (2010).

Samuel, G., Broekstra, R., Gille, F., & Lucassen, A. (2022). Public trust and trustworthiness in biobanking: The need for more reflexivity. *Biopreserv Biobank*, *20*(3), 291–296. https://doi.org/10.1089/bio.2021.0109

Samuel, G., Hardcastle, F., Broekstra, R., & Lucassen, A. (2022). Exploring how biobanks communicate the possibility of commercial access and its associated benefits and risks in participant documents. *BMC Medical Ethics*, *23*(1), 95. https://doi.org/10.1186/s12910-022-00829-1

Universal Declaration on Bioethics and Human Rights. (2006). UNESCO.

van Daal, M., & Jongsma, K. R. (2025). Navigating ethical problems of commercialization: Towards inclusive organoid research. *Personalized Medicine*, *22*(6), 473–480. https://doi.org/10.1080/17410541.2025.2564622

Walshe, J., Elphinstone, B., Nicol, D., & Taylor, M. (2024). A systematic literature review of the 'commercialisation effect' on public attitudes towards biobank and genomic data repositories. *Public Understanding of Science*, *33*(5), 548–567. https://doi.org/10.1177/09636625241230864

5 Incidental Findings in Biobanking

5.1 Introduction: Incidental Findings as a Governance Stress-Test

Biobanks increasingly function as the infrastructural backbone of genomics, precision medicine, and data-intensive biomedical research. Biological samples and associated data deposited today may be re-analysed repeatedly over extended periods as analytical tools evolve and as new disease associations gain clinical validity. In this context, the ethical question is no longer whether biobank research *can* generate findings relevant to individual participants, but rather how frequently such findings arise and what obligations they generate when they do.

Incidental findings, often discussed alongside "secondary findings" or "individual research results", occupy an ambiguous space between research and clinical care. They are "incidental" only in relation to the research objective; from the participant's perspective, the information may carry profound personal, familial, or medical consequences. This ambiguity has led contemporary scholarship to describe the return of results as part of a gradual blurring of the research-clinical boundary, where researchers increasingly encounter "clinical-esque" responsibilities despite operating within research infrastructures (Raymond et al., 2021).

The tension is particularly acute in biobanking because institutional systems are frequently designed to minimise re-contact through anonymisation or broad consent models, thereby creating structural barriers to disclosure even when ethical justification for return exists. Based on the literature on population-based genomics, this barrier is not merely technical but institutional, whereby governance architectures themselves determine whether beneficence can be operationalised or is rendered impossible (Budin-Ljøsne, 2012).

Return of results and incidental findings in biobanking are recognised as emerging ethical pressure points. This is shown in a qualitative study involving Malaysian researchers and ethics stakeholders that indicate explicit expectations that participants should be informed of clinically significant incidental

DOI: 10.4324/9781003745785-5

findings, situating this expectation within broader themes of participant rights and benefit-sharing (Azahar et al., 2023). At the same time, the same body of work highlights reliance on broad consent and the perceived insufficiency of existing national guidance in addressing consent-related ethical complexities.

Incidental findings therefore operate as a **governance stress-test** for Malaysian biobanking. They expose the limits of static consent, the practical feasibility of re-identification, the adequacy of counselling infrastructure, and the resilience of public trust. Ethical questions surrounding incidental findings are not merely technical decisions about information flow, but they are also tests of institutional accountability, cultural responsiveness, and distributive fairness in a plural social setting. International analyses increasingly frame these dilemmas not as isolated ethical puzzles but as indicators of whether research institutions are prepared to assume limited but real duties of care arising from participant entrustment (Wolf et al., 2008).

5.2 Ethical Dimensions of Incidental Findings in Biobanking

5.2.1 Definitional Complexity and Categories of Findings

One of the first governance challenges is definitional. The term "incidental finding" may encompass a wide spectrum of discoveries, ranging from clinically actionable genetic variants to probabilistic risk indicators or information of uncertain significance. Ethical discourse generally differentiates among:

- Clinically actionable findings where preventive or therapeutic interventions exist;
- Non-actionable findings with limited medical recourse;
- Variants of uncertain significance whose predictive value remains evolving;
- Familial or reproductive risk information affecting relatives who did not directly consent; and
- Identity-related or kinship information that may disrupt personal or social relationships.

The ethical implications vary across these categories, rendering blanket policies ethically inadequate. Systematic reviews of disclosure frameworks emphasise that governance must be threshold-based and context-sensitive, because analytic validity, clinical utility, and social impact are not uniform across populations or health-system capacities (Budin-Ljøsne, 2012). What counts as "clinically significant" in a high-resource health system may not translate directly into meaningful benefit in low-resource or unevenly distributed healthcare environments.

5.2.2 Autonomy, Informational Rights, and the Limits of Broad Consent

Autonomy traditionally supports disclosure, grounded in the principle that individuals have a legitimate interest in information affecting their bodily integrity and future wellbeing. However, autonomy also encompasses the right *not* to know, particularly where disclosure may cause psychological harm or conflict with personal or religious values. Ethical analysis, therefore, increasingly treats autonomy not as a simple pro-disclosure rule but as a framework requiring preference-sensitive design.

In Malaysian biobanking practice, broad consent remains common, yet it has been cautioned that broad consent may obscure material information about downstream uses and potential return of results. It has also been noted that disclosure debates are shifting from "whether to disclose" toward "under what evaluative and communicative conditions disclosure becomes respectful rather than burdensome" (Budin-Ljøsne, 2012). The ethical problem is thus not merely the absence of consent but the misalignment between participant expectations and institutional practices. When participants believe they will be informed of important discoveries, but the disclosure is prevented by institutional policies, such a scenario will jeopardise trust and legitimacy.

5.2.3 Beneficence, Non-Maleficence, and Psychological Impact

The principle of beneficence supports disclosure where information enables prevention or treatment of serious disease. However, beneficence must be balanced against non-maleficence. Disclosure of genetic risk may generate anxiety, social stigma, insurance discrimination, or familial conflict, particularly where findings are uncertain or untreatable.

A study demonstrates that participants often value transparency and acknowledgement but do not uniformly desire all categories of information. Research programmes frequently encounter barriers related to resource limitations, counselling availability, and downstream care access, particularly among low-resource participants (Raymond et al., 2021). Consequently, ethical governance must incorporate counselling, validation pathways, and culturally sensitive communication strategies. Without such infrastructure, well-intentioned disclosure policies risk may cause avoidable harm rather than tangible benefit.

5.2.4 Justice, Reciprocity, and Trust

Incidental findings also raise questions of distributive and procedural justice. Participants frequently engage in biobank research under narratives of altruism and public benefit. When research yields information that could materially benefit them, yet is withheld without transparent justification, the relationship risks appearing extractive rather than reciprocal.

It has been argued that incidental-findings management invoke reciprocity and entrustment as complementary justifications for limited disclosure duties. Participants are not merely data sources; they are also contributors to a collective enterprise and may therefore possess a presumptive entitlement to information of clear health or reproductive relevance (Wolf et al., 2008). In Malaysia's plural social context, where willingness to participate is closely linked to trust in institutions and perceived fairness, incidental-findings governance becomes inseparable from the broader social licence of biomedical research.

5.3 Legal and Policy Context in Malaysia: Governance Without a Dedicated Statute

Given Malaysia does not possess a comprehensive statute governing biobanks that provide an explicit legal mandate on incidental findings, its current governance emerges from a constellation of **soft-law instruments, sectoral legislation, and ethics-committee oversight**. One would describe the current regulatory approach as *normatively principled yet operationally fragmented.*

At the statutory level, the Personal Data Protection Act 2010 (PDPA) constitutes the primary legal safeguard for information derived from biobanking. Although the PDPA does not expressly regulate incidental findings, several provisions are indirectly relevant to disclosure governance:

- **Section 6 (General Principle)** requires that personal data be processed with consent and for lawful purposes, which becomes pertinent when identifiable genomic findings are communicated back to participants.
- **Section 40 (Security Principle)** imposes obligations to take practical steps to protect personal data from loss or misuse, shaping how coded identifiability and re-contact systems must be designed.
- **Section 129 (Transfer of Personal Data Outside Malaysia)** is particularly relevant where incidental findings emerge through foreign laboratories, requiring either adequate protection in the recipient jurisdiction or explicit data-subject consent.

These provisions establish privacy safeguards but do not create a statutory duty to return findings, thereby leaving disclosure decisions within institutional discretion.

At the policy and guideline level, the Malaysian Guidelines on the Use of Human Biological Samples for Research (2nd ed.) provide more direct ethical direction, although still in general terms. The Guidelines emphasise:

- the obligation to inform participants of "potential future uses" of samples,

- the requirement that consent documentation be sufficiently detailed to reflect foreseeable research implications, and
- the continuing role of Research Ethics Committees (RECs) in assessing participant welfare and data-handling practices.

However, the Guidelines stop short of prescribing procedural criteria for when and how incidental findings should be returned, thereby reinforcing reliance on ethics-committee interpretation rather than on uniform national standards.

Nonetheless, it can be argued that the international instruments can further shape Malaysian practice through normative influence. For instance, the World Medical Association Declaration of Helsinki (Articles 24 and 26) underscores the duty to respect participant welfare and informed consent, and these principles can be invoked by Malaysian ethics committees when evaluating disclosure decisions. Similarly, the CIOMS International Ethical Guidelines for Health-Related Research Involving Humans (Guideline 11) recognises the ethical permissibility, and in certain circumstances the desirability, of returning individual research results when they are analytically valid, clinically significant, and actionable. Meanwhile, the OECD Guidelines on Human Biobanks and Genetic Research Databases (Best Practices 6 and 9) explicitly encourage operators to develop policies on feedback of results and to clarify conditions under which individual information may be returned.

Overall, these instruments produce a regulatory environment characterised not by absence of principle, but by absence of procedural specificity. Ethical responsibility in Malaysia would emerge through layered interpretation rather than statutory mandate, inevitably creating variability across institutions. This reinforces the need for adaptive governance frameworks capable of responding to technological evolution without sacrificing participant protection.

5.4 Governance Models and Policy Options for Incidental Findings in Malaysian Biobanking

The ethical debate surrounding incidental findings has gradually shifted from whether results *may* be returned to how disclosure should be governed responsibly. In jurisdictions lacking biobank-specific statutes, governance models function as de facto regulatory instruments, translating broad ethical norms into operational practice. Malaysian institutions can draw upon both domestic guidelines and international frameworks when designing such models.

5.4.1 Tiered and Preference-Sensitive Consent Frameworks

The first proposed model would be tiered consent frameworks that operationalise the principle of autonomy recognised under Section 6 of the PDPA 2010 and reinforced by Article 26 of the Declaration of Helsinki Article. This model requires participants to be adequately informed of potential consequences of participation and enables differentiated informational preferences. Such a tiered consent model aligns with Guideline 9 of the CIOMS 2016, which encourages disclosure practices that respect individual choice without imposing unnecessary psychological burden.

Within the Malaysian context, introducing tiered consent represents an incremental reform compatible with the Malaysian Human Biological Samples Guidelines, which already mandate disclosure of foreseeable future uses. Rather than replacing broad consent, tiered mechanisms would refine it by clarifying expectations concerning return of results and thereby strengthening legitimacy.

5.4.2 Managed Re-Contact and Coded Identifiability

Traditional anonymisation practices emphasised under Section 40 (Security Principle) of the PDPA 2010 aim to protect confidentiality, while it also eliminates the possibility of beneficent disclosure. Contemporary governance models instead favour coded identifiability, whereby samples remain linkable through secure key systems under ethics-committee control.

This approach is consistent with Best Practice 5 of the OECD, which recognises that biobank custodianship entails balancing privacy with the ethical permissibility of feedback mechanisms. Internationally, Guideline 11 of CIOMS similarly acknowledges that return of clinically significant findings may justify controlled re-identification. In Malaysia, such systems must remain subject to REC oversight to ensure compliance with PDPA safeguards while preserving the institutional capacity to act beneficently.

5.4.3 Threshold-Based Return Policies

In addition, threshold-based governance could be another regulatory approach, whereby it translates abstract ethical principles into operational criteria. These policies draw conceptual support from Guideline 11 of **CIOMS** and Article 24 of the **Declaration of Helsinki**, both of which emphasise participant welfare and proportionality of risk and benefit. The **OECD Guidelines (Best Practice 6)** further recommend that biobanks clarify whether and under what circumstances individual findings may be communicated, thereby reinforcing predictability and fairness. In the Malaysian setting, threshold criteria must be locally calibrated to reflect healthcare accessibility and counselling capacity, ensuring that disclosure does not generate inequitable burdens.

5.4.4 Counselling Infrastructure and Multidisciplinary Oversight

The ethical legitimacy of disclosure depends not only on decision criteria but also on institutional capacity. Guideline 6 of CIOMS emphasises that research participants should have access to appropriate care and counselling where findings bear clinical significance. Similarly, Article 14 of the UNESCO UDBHR links biomedical advancement with social responsibility, underscoring that informational rights are inseparable from infrastructural capability.

For Malaysian biobanks, this translates into collaboration among clinical genetics services, hospital ethics committees, and public health agencies. Governance therefore extends beyond ethics-committee approval toward professional training, funding allocation, and cross-disciplinary integration.

5.4.5 Participatory and Community-Sensitive Governance

Last but not least is the participatory governance model, which resonates with Articles 18 and 19 of the UNESCO UDBHR. Such a model promotes transparency, pluralism, and public engagement in bioethical decision-making. These provisions recognise that ethical legitimacy arises not solely from procedural compliance but also from inclusive deliberation reflecting social and cultural diversity.

In Malaysia's multi-ethnic and multi-faith setting, participatory mechanisms, such as community advisory boards or stakeholder consultations, will align with the OECD's emphasis on public trust and accountability. They serve not merely as consultation tools but also as governance strategies that integrate relational ethics into institutional practice, thereby strengthening the social licence underpinning long-term biobank sustainability.

5.5 Case Studies

5.5.1 Case Study 1: The Silent Variant – Autonomy, Infrastructure, and the Right Not to Know

Case Narrative

Aisyah, a 32-year-old administrative officer living in a semi-urban district in Selangor, participates in a university-affiliated Malaysian biobank as part of a voluntary health-screening initiative. She signs a broad consent form during a community outreach programme organised by the university hospital. The consent document emphasises contribution to future research, public health advancement, and data confidentiality. It contains a brief clause stating that "clinically significant findings may be returned where appropriate", but provides no elaboration, no opt-in or opt-out mechanism, and no indication of what "appropriate" entails.

Five years later, a collaborative genomics study re-analyses archived samples using updated sequencing technology. During quality control, researchers identify that Aisyah carries a pathogenic BRCA-associated mutation linked to significantly increased lifetime risks of breast and ovarian cancer. The finding was not the primary objective of the research, but it emerges incidentally while validating gene panels for unrelated disease modelling.

The research team faces a dilemma. The variant is clinically actionable in principle, whereby screening and prophylactic interventions exist, and Aisyah's sample is coded rather than fully anonymised, meaning re-identification is technically possible but procedurally complex. The biobank lacks an established counselling unit and has no dedicated budget for participant re-contact. Furthermore, Aisyah resides in an area where access to specialised genetic services is limited, and her socioeconomic background suggests that the cost of follow-up testing may be burdensome.

An internal ethics review meeting reveals divided opinions. Some researchers argue that withholding information that could prevent life-threatening disease is morally indefensible. Others express concern that disclosing probabilistic risk without structured counselling could cause psychological harm or social stigma. A third group raises pragmatic concerns – if one participant is contacted, the biobank may be compelled to review thousands of archived samples retrospectively, stretching resources beyond feasibility.

Aisyah is unaware that the analysis has taken place. Her initial participation had been framed as a civic contribution to science rather than an ongoing relationship with the institution.

Commentary

(A) STATIC CONSENT AND EVOLVING KNOWLEDGE

The ethical difficulty in Aisyah's case arises from the mismatch between static consent structures and dynamic scientific interpretation. Malaysian governance instruments, particularly the *Malaysian Guidelines on the Use of Human Biological Samples for Research (2nd ed.)*, emphasise respect for persons as an ongoing obligation rather than as a single transactional event. Although these Guidelines do not mandate return of incidental findings, they implicitly require institutions to anticipate downstream ethical implications when designing consent language and data governance systems. The governance failure therefore lies less in the discovery itself and more in ex-ante institutional unpreparedness.

(B) LEGAL SILENCE AND ETHICAL DISCRETION

Malaysian statutory law provides limited direct guidance on incidental findings. *The Human Tissues Act 1974* is primarily concerned with removal and therapeutic use of tissues and offers little direction for living donor genomic research. However, its normative orientation that human biological material is ethically mediated rather than purely proprietary reinforces the concept of custodianship rather than ownership. In practice, this means that discretion exercised by biobanks is not morally neutral; it carries ethical weight even in the absence of explicit statutory duties.

(C) INFORMATIONAL RIGHTS UNDER THE PDPA

The *Personal Data Protection Act 2010 (PDPA)* introduces indirect relevance. Its Notice and Choice Principle and Access Principle establish expectations of transparency and participant control over personal data. Although the PDPA does not explicitly require proactive disclosure of newly generated genetic interpretations, participants may reasonably interpret these principles as entitling them to information materially affecting their health interests. The result is a regulatory grey zone where informational justice depends more on institutional policy design than on statutory command.

(D) BENEFICENCE AND INSTITUTIONAL CAPACITY

Professional and research governance instruments such as the *Malaysian Code of Responsible Conduct in Research* and the *Malaysian Guideline for Good Clinical Practice (GCP)* underscore participant welfare, integrity, and harm avoidance. These frameworks reveal a bidirectional ethical tension – disclosure without counselling may cause psychological or social harm, while non-disclosure may withhold preventable medical benefit. Beneficence, therefore, is not fulfilled through communication alone but through the presence of supportive infrastructure, such as counselling, confirmatory testing, and referral pathways.

(E) TRUST AND RELATIONAL AUTONOMY

Given public trust is a recurring theme across Malaysian and international governance instruments, it is therefore imperative for incidental findings governance to ultimately reflect relational autonomy rather than isolated individual choice. Furthermore, it is worth highlighting that participants contribute not merely biological samples but confidence in institutional fairness. The ethical question therefore becomes not only "Is disclosure required?" but "Can non-disclosure be transparently and reasonably justified?"

Key Takeaways

- **Autonomy as an ongoing obligation.**
  Consent in biobanking should be understood as a continuing ethical relationship rather than a one-time authorisation. New scientific interpretations may activate renewed informational duties.

- **Legal minimalism does not equate to ethical sufficiency.**
  The PDPA protects access and withdrawal rights but does not mandate proactive disclosure. Ethical legitimacy depends on fairness reasoning, not statutory compliance alone.
- **Beneficence requires infrastructure.**
  Disclosure without counselling, referral, or confirmatory testing risks harm. Ethical return of results must be supported by institutional capacity, not symbolic transparency.
- **Discretion carries moral weight.**
  The absence of explicit statutory duties shifts responsibility to ethics committees and institutional policies. Silence becomes an ethical decision, not a neutral default.
- **Trust is the core governance currency.**
  Incidental findings management ultimately determines whether participants perceive research as reciprocal or extractive. Transparent reasoning and visible accountability sustain long-term public trust.

5.5.2 Case Study 2: The Inherited Risk – Family, Stigma, and Relational Autonomy

Case Narrative

Ravi, a 28-year-old software engineer from Penang, enrolled in a hospital-based Malaysian biobank while accompanying his father for cardiovascular treatment. Participation was presented as a contribution to future medical research, and the consent form, similar to Aisyah's, emphasised confidentiality and scientific advancement. No explicit section addressed incidental findings or the potential familial implications of genetic discoveries.

Four years later, a genomic research collaboration identifies that Ravi carries a pathogenic mutation associated with Long QT Syndrome, a hereditary cardiac condition that increases the risk of sudden arrhythmic death. The mutation is highly penetrant and clinically actionable through lifestyle modification and medical intervention. Importantly, the condition is autosomal dominant, meaning Ravi's siblings and future children face a statistically significant risk.

When contacted by the research team under a pilot-managed re-contact protocol, Ravi reacts with visible distress. He expresses fear that disclosure within his extended family may jeopardise his younger sister's marriage prospects and create social stigma in his community. He also worries that insurance and employment opportunities could be affected if the information becomes known. Ravi therefore requests that the information remain confidential, and he declines any assistance in informing relatives.

The research team now confronts a dilemma – whether they should respect Ravi's confidentiality and autonomy or intervene in the interest of preventing foreseeable harm to biologically related family members who remain unaware of their potential risk.

Commentary

(A) RELATIONAL AUTONOMY AND FAMILIAL IMPLICATIONS

Ravi's case demonstrates that incidental findings in genomic research extend beyond individual decision-making into the relational sphere of family life. The *Malaysian Guidelines on the Use of Human Biological Samples for Research (2nd ed.)* emphasise confidentiality and respect for persons, yet they also acknowledge that research involving biological materials may generate information with wider implications than originally anticipated. Although the Guidelines do not expressly authorise third-party disclosure without consent, they embed a governance expectation that institutions anticipate familial consequences at the consent-design stage rather than addressing them only after discovery.

(B) CONFIDENTIALITY UNDER THE PDPA AND ITS LIMITS

From a statutory standpoint, the *Personal Data Protection Act 2010 (PDPA)* strongly reinforces Ravi's right to confidentiality by restricting disclosure of identifiable personal data without consent. Its structure prioritises data security, notice, and choice rather than familial risk communication. However, the PDPA does not directly address the relational nature of genetic information or the ethics of preventable harm to relatives. This creates a governance tension in which legal compliance may protect privacy while ethical reasoning simultaneously questions whether absolute silence produces informational inequity.

(C) HARM PREVENTION AND RESEARCHER ACCOUNTABILITY

Professional instruments such as the *Malaysian Code of Responsible Conduct in Research* emphasise integrity, accountability, and the avoidance of harm arising from research practices. In Ravi's situation, harm is not confined to the participant but extends to biologically connected individuals facing foreseeable medical risk. The Code does not mandate disclosure, but from the ethical point of view, researchers must be able to ethically justify institutional silence, rather than treating confidentiality as an automatic default.

(D) CULTURAL STIGMA AND SOCIAL CONSEQUENCES

In Malaysia's plural socio-cultural environment, genetic disclosure may affect marriage prospects, insurance access, and communal perception. These consequences are ethically constitutive rather than peripheral. Governance frameworks that disregard stigma, kinship expectations, and social reputation risk eroding participant trust. Ethical legitimacy emerges when counselling and communication strategies demonstrate cultural literacy, rather than assuming purely biomedical interpretations of risk.

(E) ETHICS COMMITTEES IN A STATUTORY GREY ZONE

Where statutory law remains silent, ethics committees function as the principal sites of normative interpretation. Ministry of Health governance requirements and institutional oversight structures do not resolve the confidentiality-familial risk dilemma directly, but they establish expectations of documented deliberation and justifiable reasoning. International instruments such as the *CIOMS Ethical Guidelines*, frequently cited by Malaysian regulatory instruments, recognise that exceptional disclosure to relatives may be ethically permissible where serious and preventable harm is imminent. The result is a hybrid governance landscape, whereby confidentiality is strongly protected, yet absolute silence is not ethically presumed.

Key Takeaways

- **Autonomy has relational dimensions.**
  Genetic information affects families as well as individuals. Ethical governance must recognise relational consequences without erasing participant agency.
- **Legal confidentiality and ethical finality.**
  The PDPA safeguards privacy but does not resolve preventable familial harm. Ethical reasoning must assess proportionality and fairness beyond legal compliance.
- **Harm prevention requires institutional justification.**
  Research governance instruments emphasise accountability for indirect harm. Silence must be ethically defended, not procedurally assumed.
- **Cultural context shapes ethical legitimacy.**
  Stigma, marriage prospects, and communal reputation influence how participants interpret disclosure. Culturally informed counselling is essential to sustain trust.
- **Ethics committees anchor governance where law is silent.**
  Transparent and documented deliberation drawing on both domestic guidance and international norms determines the ethical sustainability of disclosure decisions.

5.5.3 *Case Study 3: Destiny or Duty – Religious Belief, Preventive Ethics, and Moral Agency*

Case Narrative

Farid, a 41-year-old secondary school teacher from Kelantan, enrolled in a public university biobank during a community health outreach programme conducted in collaboration with a teaching hospital. Participation was framed as a contribution to scientific advancement and national health knowledge.

The consent form resembled standard broad-consent language, emphasising confidentiality and research benefit but providing minimal elaboration on incidental findings or long-term re-contact.

Several years later, genomic re-analysis identifies that Farid carries a high-risk genetic predisposition to early-onset colorectal cancer. The variant is clinically actionable, with screening and preventive interventions significantly reducing morbidity and mortality. Under a newly introduced institutional managed re-contact protocol, Farid is informed of the finding and offered referral to a clinical genetics unit.

Farid responds respectfully but declines further medical engagement. He explains that illness and longevity are matters of divine decree (*takdir*) and that pursuing invasive screening would reflect a lack of spiritual acceptance. He expresses appreciation for the information but insists that he will not act upon it. The research team now faces a dilemma – whether continued encouragement constitutes ethical responsibility or cultural insensitivity, and whether silence after disclosure satisfies their moral obligations.

Commentary

(A) MORAL AGENCY BEYOND INFORMATIONAL AUTONOMY

Farid's case shifts the governance axis from *whether disclosure is justified* to *how institutions respond after disclosure*. The ethical tension here is not informational justice but moral agency – the participant's right to interpret knowledge through religious or philosophical belief systems. Malaysian governance instruments, particularly the *Malaysian Guidelines on the Use of Human Biological Samples for Research (2nd ed.)*, emphasise respect for persons, dignity, and voluntariness as continuing obligations rather than as procedural formalities. Although the Guidelines do not explicitly address religious refusal, their framing of participant welfare and cultural sensitivity implicitly recognises that ethical legitimacy lies not in behavioural compliance but in ensuring that refusal is informed, voluntary, and free from coercion.

This position aligns with Bredenoord's analysis on the feedback of individual genetic results, which emphasises that autonomy is not exhausted by access to information but includes the freedom to decide how that information is integrated into one's life narrative (Bredenoord & van Delden, 2012). Thus, Farid's refusal does not represent ethical failure but rather the exercise of moral self-determination within a pluralistic society.

(B) PDPA AS A BOUNDARY-SETTING INSTRUMENT

From a statutory perspective, the *Personal Data Protection Act 2010 (PDPA)* reinforces participant control over personal information and subsequent engagement. The PDPA is not a clinical-decision statute, but its Notice and

Choice Principle and emphasis on consent indirectly support Farid's prerogative to decline further medical involvement. The Act functions less as a disclosure directive and more as a boundary-setting mechanism that limits institutional overreach.

Importantly, the PDPA does not require participants to act upon information received; it protects the right to disengage. This legal silence on behavioural compliance reinforces the ethical distinction between informing and persuading – a distinction central to incidental-findings literature that cautions against conflating beneficence with paternalism.

(C) BENEFICENCE VERSUS CULTURAL NON-MALEFICENCE

Professional governance frameworks deepen this analysis. The *Malaysian Code of Responsible Conduct in Research* stresses integrity, accountability, and avoidance of harm arising from research practices, including harm produced through disrespectful engagement. In Farid's context, harm may arise not from silence but from pressurised persuasion that undermines spiritual conviction or personal dignity.

Similarly, the *Malaysian Guideline for Good Clinical Practice (GCP)* emphasises voluntariness and the right to withdraw or decline intervention without prejudice. Although designed primarily for interventional trials, its principles are routinely invoked by ethics committees reviewing genomic research. International literature on return of results, including low-resource participant studies, consistently demonstrates that well-intentioned disclosure without cultural sensitivity can generate alienation rather than empowerment. Thus, beneficence must be balanced against cultural non-maleficence.

(D) ETHICS COMMITTEES AS CULTURAL MEDIATORS

Ministry of Health research governance requirements underscore that decisions following incidental findings should be justified through ethics-committee deliberation, not individual investigator discretion. Ethics committees in Malaysia could draw upon CIOMS guidance, which recognises the right to refuse health-related information or intervention provided refusal is informed and does not endanger others.

In Farid's case, the legitimacy of institutional action depends less on the outcome than on the visibility of reasoned, documented, and culturally literate deliberation. Ethics committees therefore function as mediators between biomedical rationality and plural moral frameworks rather than as enforcement bodies.

(E) TRUST THROUGH RESPECT RATHER THAN COMPLIANCE

Trust is sustained when institutions demonstrate respect for informed refusal, even where medical benefit is evident. Farid's case illustrates that honouring moral agency can be as ethically significant as returning clinically actionable information.

Key Takeaways

- **Autonomy includes moral and spiritual interpretation.**
  Autonomy in genomic contexts is not limited to informational access but encompasses the participant's right to interpret health knowledge through religious, philosophical, or cultural frameworks. Ethical governance in plural societies therefore requires recognition that refusal may represent reflective moral agency rather than ignorance or resistance.
- **Disclosure reconfigures institutional responsibility.**
  Returning incidental findings does not end ethical obligations; it transforms them from information delivery to respectful post-disclosure engagement. Institutions must ensure that refusal is informed and voluntary while avoiding coercive or paternalistic follow-up that undermines dignity.
- **Cultural sensitivity is an element of non-maleficence.**
  Harm in biomedical governance is not exclusively physical or psychological. It may also arise from cultural or spiritual alienation. Ethical practice therefore requires culturally literate counselling and communication strategies that acknowledge belief systems without compromising scientific accuracy.
- **Ethics committees function as mediators of moral diversity.**
  Where statutory law provides limited direction, ethics committees become the principal sites of interpretive governance. Their legitimacy depends on transparent reasoning, documentation, and the capacity to balance biomedical benefit with plural moral values rather than enforcing uniform outcomes.
- **Trust emerges from respect rather than persuasion.**
  Long-term public confidence in biobanking institutions is sustained when participants perceive that their dignity and belief systems are honoured, even when medical advice is declined. Respectful acknowledgement of informed refusal can reinforce institutional legitimacy more effectively than successful persuasion can.

5.5.4 Case Study 4: The Uncertain Gene – Scientific Validity, Over-Disclosure, and the Limits of Beneficence

Case Narrative

Mei Ling, a 35-year-old accountant from Kuala Lumpur, participated in a university biobank through a workplace health initiative. Participation was presented as a contribution to national medical research and long-term public health advancement. The consent form followed a standard broad-consent template, emphasising confidentiality and data security but providing limited clarification on incidental findings or the categories of information that might be returned.

Several years later, genomic re-analysis identifies a **Variant of Uncertain Significance (VUS)** associated with a neurological disorder. The variant has inconclusive predictive value and no established preventive or therapeutic intervention. The research team is divided; a junior researcher recommends disclosure in the name of transparency, while other senior clinicians caution that the information lacks clinical actionability and may generate unnecessary anxiety.

When Mei Ling is tentatively informed that an indeterminate genetic signal exists but that its medical meaning is unclear, she begins searching online forums and medical blogs. Conflicting information heightens her anxiety, leading her to consider expensive private neurological screenings and additional insurance coverage despite repeated reassurances that the variant has no confirmed clinical implication. Simultaneously, the biobank's counselling unit warns that returning all uncertain findings could overwhelm limited support resources and create widespread misunderstanding among participants.

The ethics committee must therefore decide whether disclosure of uncertain findings constitutes empowerment through transparency or avoidable psychological and social harm produced by premature scientific communication.

Commentary

(A) ANALYTICAL VALIDITY AND THE ETHICS OF SCIENTIFIC THRESHOLDS

Unlike the earlier cases centred on autonomy, infrastructure, or belief systems, Mei Ling's situation foregrounds epistemic uncertainty. International genomic ethics scholarship, particularly the work of Bredenoord on feedback of individual genetic results and the evidence-based frameworks advanced by the ClinGen Actionability Working Group, consistently emphasises that disclosure should generally be limited to findings meeting thresholds of analytic validity, clinical significance, and clinical actionability (Bredenoord & van Delden, 2012; Webber et al., 2018). These criteria are not merely technical filters; they function as ethical safeguards against conflating informational abundance with meaningful benefit.

Although Malaysian statutes do not codify such thresholds, Malaysian ethics committees could rely on CIOMS guidance and comparative genomic governance frameworks when evaluating disclosure policies. The absence of statutory specificity therefore does not imply ethical indifference; rather, it places greater weight on institutional threshold-setting as a governance responsibility.

(B) NON-MALEFICENCE AND PSYCHOLOGICAL HARM

Managing incidental findings in human subjects research that are uncertain or with low-validity results without delivering tangible clinical benefit may produce anxiety, stigma, and lead to misinformed medical decision-making.

Mei Ling's escalating concern illustrates how indeterminate disclosure can transform speculative data into perceived diagnosis.

Malaysian professional governance instruments, particularly the *Malaysian Code of Responsible Conduct in Research*, embed harm-avoidance principles that extend beyond physical injury to psychological and social consequences. Ethical governance therefore requires that non-maleficence be interpreted broadly, recognising that over-disclosure may constitute harm rather than transparency.

(C) INFORMATIONAL RIGHTS AND THE PDPA: THE RIGHT NOT TO BE OVER-INFORMED

The *Personal Data Protection Act 2010 (PDPA)* affirms participants' rights to access and control personal data, yet it does not compel institutions to generate or communicate speculative interpretations. This distinction is crucial. Informational rights are not equivalent to a duty to transmit every piece of uncertain knowledge.

Research participants have the right not to receive indeterminate or low-utility information, particularly where such disclosure lacks proportional benefit. In this sense, the PDPA operates as a framework for informational autonomy rather than informational maximalism, reinforcing that ethical governance involves selective, reasoned communication rather than indiscriminate disclosure.

(D) THRESHOLD-BASED GOVERNANCE AND INSTITUTIONAL PREDICTABILITY

Contemporary genomic governance literature advocates threshold-based return policies as a means of balancing transparency with scientific responsibility. Evidence-based actionability frameworks, such as those produced by ClinGen and discussed extensively in international policy debates, provide structured criteria for determining which findings merit return (Webber et al., 2018). Rather than ad hoc decision-making, threshold-based governance signals that disclosure decisions are anchored in scientific evidence and ethical proportionality.

(E) TRUST, SCIENTIFIC INTEGRITY, AND INSTITUTIONAL CREDIBILITY

Over-communication of uncertain findings may later be interpreted as alarmism or institutional defensiveness, thereby weakening participant confidence. Conversely, transparent restraint, when accompanied by clear explanation and accessible policies, reinforces the perception that institutions act as prudent stewards of knowledge rather than indiscriminate transmitters of uncertainty.

Key Takeaways

- **Not all findings ethically merit disclosure.**
  Clinical actionability, analytic validity, and evidentiary reliability constitute ethically relevant thresholds for returning results. Ethical governance distinguishes between medically meaningful information and speculative data to prevent the dilution of responsibility through indiscriminate transparency.
- **Transparency without certainty may produce avoidable harm.**
  Disclosure of indeterminate variants can generate anxiety, social stigma, and unnecessary financial or medical decision-making. Ethical proportionality requires balancing openness with the potential psychological and social consequences of uncertain knowledge.
- **Informational rights include the right not to receive indeterminate knowledge.**
  Participant autonomy encompasses both access to meaningful information and protection from low-utility or speculative disclosure. Respecting this dimension aligns with both PDPA principles and international genomic ethics scholarship.
- **Threshold-based policies promote fairness and predictability.**
  Institutional criteria grounded in evidence-based actionability frameworks provide consistency, defensibility, and transparency. Such policies help avoid arbitrary disclosure decisions and strengthen participant confidence in governance processes.
- **Trust depends on scientific integrity as much as openness.**
  Public confidence in biobanking institutions is reinforced when disclosure practices reflect careful scientific judgement rather than defensive over-communication. Responsible restraint, when transparently justified, can be as ethically significant as disclosure itself.

5.6 Concluding Reflections

This chapter has argued that incidental findings in biobanking are not peripheral anomalies but rather structural features of contemporary biomedical research. As genomic technologies mature and analytical capacities expand, the likelihood that archived biological materials will yield clinically or personally significant information correspondingly increases. The ethical challenge, therefore, is not the management of rare exceptions but the governance of an increasingly predictable dimension of research practice. Incidental findings operate as a stress-test of institutional preparedness, exposing the strengths and weaknesses of consent architectures, counselling infrastructures, oversight mechanisms, and cultural responsiveness within Malaysia's evolving biomedical ecosystem.

The case studies demonstrate that incidental-findings governance unfolds along a continuum of relational complexity rather than within a single ethical frame. At the individual level, the dilemma of disclosure versus silence reveals the limits of static consent and underscores autonomy as temporal and revisitable rather than fixed at the moment of enrolment. At the familial level, genetic relationality disrupts the assumption that personal data belong exclusively to one individual, compelling institutions to balance confidentiality with the prevention of foreseeable harm to relatives. At the cultural and religious level, the interpretation of knowledge itself becomes ethically constitutive, reminding governance structures that biomedical rationality operates within plural moral worlds rather than in a value-neutral space. At the institutional level, the focus shifts from participant choice to systemic accountability, where foreseeability, proportionality, and infrastructural capacity become the principal benchmarks of ethical legitimacy.

Across these dimensions, Malaysian regulatory and policy instruments reveal a distinctive pattern best described as **legal silence accompanied by ethical expectation**. Statutes such as the Personal Data Protection Act 2010 establish important safeguards concerning confidentiality, consent, and informational control, yet stop short of imposing an explicit statutory duty to return incidental findings. The Human Tissues Act 1974 provides a custodial orientation toward bodily materials without detailed operational guidance for living-donor genomic research. Consequently, the practical governance of incidental findings rests largely on soft-law instruments, research-ethics committee deliberation, ministerial guidelines, and institutional policies. This hybrid environment does not diminish ethical responsibility; rather, it intensifies reliance on deliberative governance – the visible, documented, and reasoned processes through which institutions justify decisions in the absence of rigid legislative command.

A central lesson emerging from this chapter is that incidental-findings governance cannot be reduced to a binary rule of disclosure or non-disclosure. Such reductionism obscures the layered terrain in which participant welfare, cultural context, infrastructural feasibility, scientific validity, and distributive justice intersect. Effective governance therefore requires **policy architecture** – an integrated system that may include tiered or preference-sensitive consent, managed re-contact pathways, clinically informed actionability thresholds, counselling and referral capacity, multidisciplinary oversight, and periodic policy review. These mechanisms do not eliminate ethical tension. Instead, they convert tension from an unpredictable crisis into a foreseeable and manageable element of institutional practice.

Equally significant is the role of trust as the foundational currency of biobanking. Participants contribute biological materials under narratives of altruism, solidarity, and collective benefit. When incidental findings are handled opaquely or without justification, institutions risk eroding this trust, thereby weakening both participation rates and the broader social licence of biomedical research. Conversely, governance frameworks that emphasise reciprocity, cultural literacy, transparency, and reasoned accountability strengthen the relational contract between participant and institution. Trust is not sustained by the perfection of outcomes, which are often scientifically uncertain, but by the coherence and fairness of decision-making processes.

From a Malaysian perspective, the absence of a dedicated statutory regime on incidental findings should not be interpreted solely as regulatory deficiency, but also as space for **adaptive governance innovation**. The existing network of national guidelines, professional codes, ethics-committee structures, and institutional standard-operating procedures already provides a normative foundation upon which more explicit and harmonised policies may be constructed. What is required is not necessarily immediate legislative intervention, but gradual convergence around shared principles of proportionality, transparency, participant-centred reasoning, and contextual sensitivity. Such convergence can reduce institutional variability while preserving the flexibility necessary for a rapidly evolving scientific domain.

Ultimately, incidental findings compel biobanks to confront their dual identity; that is, they are simultaneously repositories of biological data and stewards of human trust. The management of unexpected knowledge reveals whether institutions perceive participants as passive data sources or as continuing moral stakeholders in the research enterprise. The ethical sustainability of Malaysian biobanking will depend less on the existence of rigid legal mandates than on the cultivation of governance cultures that recognise responsibility as relational, anticipatory, and reflexive. In this sense, incidental findings are not merely informational by-products of research; they are ethical mirrors reflecting the maturity of institutional accountability and the depth of commitment to participant dignity in Malaysia's biomedical future.

References

Azahar, A., Mohd Yusof, A. N., & Azhar, Z. I. (2023). A preliminary study to explore the informed consent approach and the ethical challenges in the Malaysian biobanking for research. *Asian Bioethics Review*, *15*(2), 141–154. https://doi.org/10.1007/s41649-022-00229-y

Bredenoord, A. L., & van Delden, J. J. (2012). Research ethics in genomics research: Feedback of individual genetic data to research participants. In *Human medical research: Ethical, legal and socio-cultural aspects* (pp. 127–136). Springer.

Budin-Ljøsne, I. (2012). A review of ethical frameworks for the disclosure of individual research results in population-based genetic and genomic research. *Research Ethics*, *8*(1), 25–42.

Raymond, M. B., Cooper, K. E., Parker, L. S., & Bonham, V. L. (2021). Practices and attitudes toward returning genomic research results to low-resource research participants. *Public Health Genomics*, *24*(5–6), 241–252. https://karger.com/phg/article-pdf/24/5-6/241/3736870/000516782.pdf

Webber, E. M., Hunter, J. E., Biesecker, L. G., Buchanan, A. H., Clarke, E. V., Currey, E., Dagan-Rosenfeld, O., Lee, K., Lindor, N. M., & Martin, C. L. (2018). Evidence-based assessments of clinical actionability in the context of secondary findings: Updates from ClinGen's actionability working group. *Human Mutation*, *39*(11), 1677–1685. https://pmc.ncbi.nlm.nih.gov/articles/PMC6211797/

Wolf, S. M., Lawrenz, F. P., Nelson, C. A., Kahn, J. P., Cho, M. K., Clayton, E. W., Fletcher, J. G., Georgieff, M. K., Hammerschmidt, D., & Hudson, K. (2008). Managing incidental findings in human subjects research: Analysis and recommendations. *Journal of Law, Medicine & Ethics*, *36*(2), 219–248.

6 International Data Sharing and Cross-Border Collaboration

6.1 The Importance of International Data Sharing in Biobanking

International data sharing has become an indispensable structural feature of contemporary biobanking rather than a discretionary enhancement. The scientific logic is straightforward; that is, genomic research requires scale, diversity, and statistical power that no single institution or nation can independently provide. However, the ethical and governance implications are considerably more complex. Where earlier chapters examined *value generation* (commercialisation) and *information return* (incidental findings), this chapter addresses the third structural pressure point of modern biobanking, which is the mobility of data and samples across jurisdictions.

Global collaborative infrastructures such as the UK Biobank and multinational cohort networks demonstrate that pooled datasets dramatically accelerate discovery, particularly for rare diseases and polygenic conditions. Yet international collaboration is not merely about scale, but it is also about representation. The persistent over-representation of European ancestry populations in genomic databases has been identified as a systemic ethical and scientific problem in a study by Sirugo et al. (2019), which argues that limited population diversity produces both epistemic bias and inequitable clinical translation. Cross-border collaboration therefore serves not only scientific efficiency but also distributive justice, provided that inclusion does not become extractive.

At the same time, empirical work on public attitudes indicates that willingness to share genomic data internationally is conditional rather than absolute. The multinational survey study by Middleton et al. (2020) demonstrates that trust in institutions, transparency of governance, and perceived social benefit strongly influence participant willingness. Participants are generally supportive of data sharing for medical research, but they are markedly more cautious when commercial entities or foreign governments are involved. This reveals that international data sharing is ethically sustainable only when institutional legitimacy and accountability mechanisms are visible.

DOI: 10.4324/9781003745785-6

From a governance perspective, international data sharing has also catalysed the emergence of global standard-setting bodies. The policy and technical frameworks developed by the Global Alliance for Genomics and Health in Rehm et al. (2021) emphasise interoperability, responsible access, and federated data architectures that permit analysis without wholesale data export. These models seek to balance openness with sovereignty, signalling a shift away from purely centralised data repositories toward distributed governance systems.

In the Malaysian context, participation in multinational consortia such as the Asia Cohort Consortium and collaborations involving The Malaysian Cohort Project reflects national recognition that scientific competitiveness and public-health advancement depend on international integration. However, as later sections illustrate, such participation must be matched by robust ethical and legal frameworks capable of preserving participant trust, cultural sensitivity, and national data sovereignty.

6.2 Ethical Issues in Cross-Border Data Sharing

Cross-border data sharing magnifies ethical dilemmas already present in domestic biobanking by introducing jurisdictional plurality, cultural divergence, and asymmetrical institutional power. Four recurrent ethical themes emerge across international scholarship and regulatory discourse: privacy, consent, equity, and governance accountability.

6.2.1 Privacy and Re-Identifiability Risks

Protecting participant privacy becomes substantially more complex once genomic and health data cross national borders. Although anonymisation and coding are frequently invoked as safeguards, contemporary scholarship increasingly questions their sufficiency. The legal-technical analysis by Shabani and Marelli (2019) demonstrates that genomic datasets remain intrinsically re-identifiable when cross-linked with auxiliary information, challenging the assumption that de-identification equates to anonymity. This insight is particularly significant for international data sharing, where multiple datasets, registries, and analytical tools may be combined across jurisdictions.

Privacy risks are therefore not solely technical but structural. They are amplified by disparities in data-protection regimes. The European Union's General Data Protection Regulation (GDPR) imposes stringent conditions on cross-border data transfer, whereas other jurisdictions rely on sectoral or institutional safeguards. These differences create ethical tension between scientific openness and informational security.

Emerging governance tools attempt to mitigate these risks through structured access mechanisms rather than with unrestricted sharing. The computational governance framework described by Lawson et al. (2021) illustrates how machine-readable access conditions can operationalise ethical restrictions at scale. Such approaches signal a shift from binary access/no-access models toward nuanced, condition-based data stewardship.

For Malaysian institutions, these concerns intersect with the Personal Data Protection Act 2010 (PDPA), particularly Section 129 on cross-border data transfer, which requires comparable safeguards or explicit consent ("Personal Data Protection Act", 2010). Although the PDPA focuses primarily on identifiability and security, ethical governance increasingly demands broader transparency regarding downstream use and data linkage potential.

6.2.2 Informed Consent and Participant Autonomy

As highlighted earlier, consent in international data sharing cannot be reduced to the presence of a signed document. Instead, it must be understood as an evolving relational process. Traditional broad-consent models offer administrative efficiency but risk obscuring downstream uses, particularly international collaborations and commercial partnerships.

Scholarly evaluation of alternative consent architectures is extensively discussed in a study by Prictor et al. (2020), which proposes digitally mediated, ongoing participant engagement as a means of preserving autonomy over time. Dynamic consent enhances responsiveness, but it also introduces infrastructural and digital-literacy challenges, especially in low- and middle-income contexts, as argued by Abdul Aziz and Mohd Yusof (2019).

Complementing this perspective, clinical-ethics scholarship by Riggs et al. (2019) emphasises the necessity of explicit explanation regarding international data flows, third-party access, and future research scope. These works collectively highlight that meaningful consent depends on comprehension, cultural translation, and ongoing communication rather than one-time formalities.

Within Malaysia, the Guidelines on the Use of Human Biological Samples for Research implicitly support transparency and foreseeability in consent processes, although they do not mandate granular international-transfer clauses (Malaysia Ministry of Health, 2025). Ethics committees therefore play a pivotal interpretive role in determining whether existing consent adequately covers cross-border sharing.

6.2.3 Equity, Inclusion, and Benefit-Sharing

International collaboration risks reproducing historical asymmetries unless explicit equity mechanisms are embedded. Concerns regarding "data extraction" and "helicopter research" are particularly salient for LMICs contributing biological materials to wealthier research ecosystems.

The policy analysis presented in a study that looked into the best practices of sharing health research data from LMIC settings by Bull et al. (2015)

underscores reciprocity, capacity building, and shared authorship as central ethical requirements. Data sharing is framed not merely as technical exchange but as a relational partnership demanding recognition of contribution and mutual benefit.

Similarly, the governance framework described by Tindana et al. (2019) in developing the H3Africa model for an ethical data sharing demonstrates how regional ethics networks can mitigate structural inequities through collaborative oversight, training, and policy harmonisation. Although geographically distinct, the H3Africa model offers conceptual parallels for Southeast Asian governance development.

For Malaysia, equity concerns are not limited to international disparities but also extend to internal rural-urban and indigenous-community dimensions. Ethical data sharing therefore intersects with distributive justice, representation, and long-term infrastructural investment.

6.2.4 Governance and Accountability Across Borders

Perhaps the most complex challenge in international data sharing is accountability. Once data traverse multiple jurisdictions, responsibility becomes diffused unless it is explicitly delineated. Governance mechanisms increasingly rely on layered soft-law instruments, institutional agreements, and technical standards.

The international policy architecture articulated by Rehm et al. (2021) emphasises harmonised technical standards combined with policy frameworks addressing consent, security, and data access. Rather than replacing national law, these standards function as interoperable ethical scaffolding.

Within Malaysia, governance responsibility is distributed across multiple instruments:

- **Personal Data Protection Act 2010 (PDPA)** – confidentiality and cross-border transfer safeguards
- **Malaysian Guidelines on the Use of Human Biological Samples for Research** – consent, storage, and transfer expectations
- **Malaysian Code of Responsible Conduct in Research** – integrity, transparency, and accountability
- **Medical Research and Ethics Committee (MREC) oversight** – protocol approval and monitoring

These instruments collectively form a hybrid governance ecosystem that depends heavily on ethics-committee deliberation rather than on statutory prescription. International collaboration therefore requires not merely legal compliance but normative convergence, where participating institutions align ethical expectations even when legal systems differ.

6.3 Legal and Regulatory Frameworks Governing Cross-Border Data Sharing

The legal landscape for international biobank collaboration is inherently plural. No single treaty comprehensively governs genomic data exchange, resulting in reliance on overlapping domestic statutes, regional regulations, and international soft-law frameworks.

At the international level, the GDPR represents the most stringent contemporary data-protection regime, particularly regarding adequacy assessments and transfer safeguards. In contrast, jurisdictions such as the United States employ sector-specific regulation rather than unified data-privacy statutes. These disparities necessitate contractual instruments such as Data Transfer Agreements and Material Transfer Agreements to bridge regulatory gaps.

Complementing formal law, international policy guidance plays an increasingly influential role. The OECD instrument, Recommendation of the Council on Enhancing Access to and Sharing of Data (OECD/LEGAL/0463), articulates the principles of proportionality, transparency, security, and public engagement, providing non-binding yet widely referenced standards for responsible data use (OECD, 2025). Similarly, GA4GH frameworks emphasise interoperability and federated analysis as technical-ethical solutions to cross-border governance complexity (Rehm et al., 2021).

Within Malaysia, regulation remains fragmented but evolving:

- **Personal Data Protection Act 2010 (PDPA)** – cross-border transfer conditions and sensitive-data safeguards
- **Human Tissues Act 1974** – limited applicability but establishes custodial orientation toward biological materials
- **Guidelines on the Use of Human Biological Samples for Research** – consent and ethical transfer expectations
- **Medical Research and Ethics Committee (MREC)** – oversight authority in Ministry of Health facilities

Although Malaysia lacks a dedicated biobank statute, it can be said that the existing framework reflects a principled yet operationally incomplete governance model. The regulatory emphasis remains on confidentiality and consent rather than comprehensive cross-border accountability. Consequently, ethical sustainability depends significantly on institutional policy development and ethics-committee interpretation rather than statutory mandate.

From a forward-looking perspective, international collaboration increasingly demands regulatory interoperability rather than uniformity. Therefore, Malaysia's participation in global biobank networks positions it to influence emerging standards, but also necessitates continued refinement of domestic governance instruments to preserve participant trust, cultural sensitivity, and data sovereignty.

6.4 Case Studies

6.4.1 Case Study 1: The Data Transfer Quandary

Case Narrative

A Malaysian university-affiliated biobank enters into a collaborative agreement with a genomics institute in East Asia to participate in a multi-centre diabetes research consortium. The partnership promises access to advanced sequencing infrastructure, international co-authorship opportunities, and enhanced institutional visibility. Under a Memorandum of Understanding (MoU) signed at the institutional level, biospecimens and associated clinical datasets from approximately 3,000 Malaysian participants are transferred to the overseas partner.

The original consent forms, however, were drafted nearly a decade earlier. They authorised use of samples for "future health-related research" but contained no explicit reference to international data transfer, long-term foreign storage, or commercial analytics partnerships. The research team interprets the consent language as sufficiently broad, reasoning that anonymisation and encryption provide adequate safeguards. The transfer proceeds through secure digital channels, and biospecimens are shipped in coded form.

Two years later, a Malaysian civil-society digital-rights organisation publishes a report indicating that the overseas partner has integrated the dataset into a subscription-based analytics platform used by pharmaceutical companies for drug-target modelling. Although direct identifiers were not included, metadata fields, such as ethnicity, regional health indicators, and age bands, enable partial re-identification when cross-linked with publicly accessible registries. Participants become aware of the situation through media coverage rather than institutional communication, and they express discomfort, asserting that their data were exported without meaningful understanding of downstream commercial use.

The Malaysian institution maintains that all procedures complied with existing ethics approval and that anonymisation satisfied legal standards. The public debate consequently shifts from *legal compliance* to *ethical legitimacy*, raising questions about jurisdictional accountability, data sovereignty, and the moral limits of broad consent in cross-border data ecosystems.

Commentary

(A) CONSENT SPECIFICITY AND POST-CONSENT DRIFT

The central ethical issue is not the existence of international collaboration itself but the interpretive expansion of consent beyond participants' reasonable expectations. Broad consent language, "future health research", may satisfy procedural efficiency, yet its ethical robustness diminishes when extended to foreign commercial analytics platforms.

The Malaysian Guidelines on the Use of Human Biological Samples for Research (2nd ed.) emphasise that consent should reflect *foreseeable* uses of biological materials, including data-sharing arrangements and storage conditions. Although the Guidelines do not prohibit broad consent, they implicitly caution against post-hoc interpretive drift that qualitatively alters the meaning of participation (Malaysia Ministry of Health, 2025). Ethical legitimacy therefore hinges less on textual breadth than on participant comprehension and expectation alignment.

International scholarship reinforces this concern. Analyses of consent design in genomic data sharing, such as the work by Riggs et al. (2019), demonstrate that international transfer and commercial analytics constitute distinct informational categories requiring explicit explanation rather than implied authorisation.

(B) INFORMATIONAL SOVEREIGNTY AND INSTITUTIONAL STEWARDSHIP

Cross-border transfer transforms stewardship into a jurisdictionally dispersed responsibility. Once datasets leave Malaysian territory, institutional control over interpretive use and data linkage becomes attenuated.

The Personal Data Protection Act 2010 (PDPA), particularly Section 129, restricts cross-border data transfer unless the receiving jurisdiction provides comparable data-protection safeguards or explicit participant consent is obtained ("Personal Data Protection Act", 2010). Although anonymisation reduces legal exposure, it does not extinguish ethical concern where re-identification remains technically feasible. Contemporary legal-technical analysis, including the work by Shabani and Marelli (2019), illustrates that genomic datasets retain intrinsic identifiability when triangulated with auxiliary information.

Ethically, the issue extends beyond privacy into informational sovereignty – the participants' expectation that their data remain governed within a familiar normative and legal ecosystem. Jurisdictional drift therefore alters not only legal oversight but also moral context, often without participant awareness.

(C) COMMERCIAL REPURPOSING AND VALUE RE-INTERPRETATION

The incorporation of the dataset into a commercial analytics platform represents a transformation of research purpose. What began as academic collaboration evolves into value extraction.

The Malaysian Code of Responsible Conduct in Research underscores integrity, transparency, and accountability in data stewardship, implying that downstream commercial repurposing should be either explicitly consented to or institutionally justified through participant-centred reasoning. Ethical tension arises not from the generation of commercial value per se, but from the re-framing of altruistic contribution into profit-oriented infrastructure without reciprocal communication or benefit articulation.

Empirical work on public attitudes and perceptions of genomic data sharing, including the work by Middleton et al. (2020), indicates that participants generally differentiate between public-interest research and commercial exploitation. The ethical fragility therefore lies in *value reinterpretation without narrative continuity.*

(D) TRACEABILITY, TRANSPARENCY, AND RELATIONAL ACCOUNTABILITY

A critical governance deficiency in this scenario is the absence of traceability mechanisms. Participants learned of international and commercial use through media exposure rather than institutional communication.

Ministry of Health research-governance circulars and ethics-committee expectations emphasise accountability beyond initial project approval, implying that cross-border data sharing entails ongoing relational obligations. Ethical governance requires not merely secure transfer but visible data trajectories, which includes registries of data access, periodic reporting, and accessible communication channels.

Scholarly proposals, such as the one proposed by Lawson et al. (2021), suggest that computational governance tools can enhance transparency by embedding access conditions directly into data infrastructures. Such mechanisms illustrate how technical design and ethical accountability can converge.

(E) INTERNATIONAL NORMATIVE ALIGNMENT AND SOFT-LAW CONVERGENCE

International ethical frameworks function as interpretive bridges in contexts of legal asymmetry. Instruments such as the OECD Recommendation (OECD, 2025) and policy standards articulated by Rehm et al. (2021) emphasise proportionality, participant engagement, and harmonised access governance.

Although they are non-binding, these frameworks should be referenced by Malaysian ethics committees when domestic statutory provisions are silent. Their significance lies in cultivating normative convergence rather than imposing uniform law, aligning expectations, providing for transparency practices, and promoting accountability norms across jurisdictions.

Key Takeaways

- **Broad consent does not constitute blanket authorisation.**
  Malaysian research guidelines recognise broad consent as administratively efficient but ethically contingent. International transfer and commercial analytics represent qualitative shifts that participants may not reasonably

anticipate, necessitating explicit disclosure or supplementary notification mechanisms.

- **Legal anonymisation does not exhaust ethical responsibility.**
  Compliance with PDPA identifiability standards provides important safeguards but does not eliminate re-identification risk or contextual reinterpretation. Ethical legitimacy requires transparency, proportionality, and participant-centred fairness beyond technical compliance.
- **Commercial repurposing demands reciprocity and narrative continuity.**
  The Malaysian Code of Responsible Conduct in Research signals that integrity in data stewardship includes clarity regarding downstream value generation. Participant trust is sustained when institutions articulate how commercial benefits align with societal or participant interests rather than appearing extractive.
- **Traceability is core ethical infrastructure.**
  Ethics-committee oversight and Ministry of Health governance expectations extend beyond initial approval. Cross-border collaboration therefore requires visible data-flow registers, reporting mechanisms, and accessible communication channels that allow participants to understand where their data reside and how they are used.
- **International collaboration requires normative convergence, not mere technical agreement.**
  Soft-law instruments such as OECD and GA4GH frameworks serve as ethical bridges where legal asymmetry exists. Sustainable cross-border governance depends on shared principles of transparency, accountability, and participant engagement rather than contractual or technical safeguards alone.

6.4.2 Case Study 2: The Indigenous Genomics Export and Digital Colonialism

Case Narrative

A national population-genomics initiative is launched in Malaysia with the objective of mapping genetic diversity across major ethnic and sub-ethnic groups to support long-term public-health planning and precision-medicine research. The project receives public funding, institutional ethics approval, and media endorsement as a symbol of national scientific progress. Participation is framed as a civic contribution to the country's biomedical future.

Several Orang Asli communities in Peninsular Malaysia are recruited through mobile research teams. Information sessions are conducted in Bahasa Malaysia with limited oral translation into Indigenous dialects. Participants are informed that their samples will support "health and ancestry research", and assurances of confidentiality are repeatedly emphasised. No detailed explanation is provided regarding international data transfer, long-term foreign storage, or potential commercial partnerships.

Three years later, investigative journalists reveal that anonymised genomic datasets from the initiative were shared with a private biotechnology company in the United States developing commercial ancestry-testing services and population-heritage algorithms. Although the dataset was coded and direct identifiers were removed, the company's marketing materials reference "rare Southeast Asian indigenous genetic markers", triggering widespread public criticism.

Community leaders from the Orang Asli villages assert that their biological heritage has been appropriated without meaningful consultation or collective consent. They describe the incident as a form of *biocolonialism* and "digital extraction", arguing that their genetic identity has been transformed into commercial value without cultural recognition, community representation, or tangible benefit. The Malaysian research institution responds that all transfers complied with anonymisation standards and institutional ethics approval. The controversy consequently shifts from procedural legality to questions of collective dignity, cultural sovereignty, and structural power imbalance in cross-border genomic research.

Commentary

(A) COLLECTIVE IDENTITY AND THE LIMITS OF INDIVIDUAL CONSENT

This case foregrounds the structural inadequacy of purely individual consent models where biological data simultaneously function as markers of collective cultural identity. While each participant signed an individual consent form, the derived genomic dataset was subsequently interpreted as representative of an entire indigenous population.

The Malaysian Guidelines on the Use of Human Biological Samples for Research (2nd ed.) emphasise respect for persons, cultural sensitivity, and participant welfare, implicitly acknowledging that biological materials may embody communal as well as individual significance (Malaysia Ministry of Health, 2025). However, the Guidelines do not establish explicit mechanisms for community-level authorisation or collective veto rights. The ethical difficulty therefore arises not from direct procedural violation but from governance omission, whereby individual authorisation was treated as sufficient for decisions affecting collective identity.

As highlighted by Sirugo et al. (2019) in their comparative governance literature, under-represented populations often experience research not merely as participation but as identity representation, magnifying the ethical weight of consent beyond individual scope.

(B) DIGITAL COLONIALISM AND STRUCTURAL POWER ASYMMETRY

The language of "digital colonialism" emerges when biological data from marginalised communities are extracted, analysed, and monetised by more technologically and economically powerful actors without reciprocal participation or control. Although the Malaysian institution may not have intended exploitation, the cross-border transfer reproduced asymmetrical knowledge flows in which analytic authority and commercial value migrated outward while cultural ownership and interpretive control remained external.

In Indigenous genomic contexts, harm manifests not solely through privacy breach but also through symbolic dispossession, which includes the perception that communal heritage has been commodified without recognition or agency. Ethical harm here is reputational, cultural, and historical rather than purely informational. As highlighted in their work on ethical data sharing in LMIC settings, Bull et al. (2015) warn that technical compliance without structural equity risks reproducing extractive research dynamics.

(C) CULTURAL SOVEREIGNTY, DATA PROTECTION, AND REGULATORY GAPS

The controversy also exposes the distinction between data protection and cultural sovereignty.

The Personal Data Protection Act 2010 (PDPA) focuses on identifiability, consent, and data security, providing limited guidance on collective cultural rights, group intellectual interests, or identity representation. Even when personal identifiers are removed, communal identity embedded within genomic datasets remains ethically salient ("Personal Data Protection Act", 2010). Regulatory compliance with anonymisation standards may therefore coexist with perceived cultural violation.

This gap illustrates that privacy law alone cannot address the ethical dimensions of Indigenous genomic research. Governance frameworks centred exclusively on personal data fail to capture the relational and symbolic meaning of biological heritage, thereby appearing technically compliant yet morally insufficient.

(D) OVERSIGHT, CONSULTATION, AND COMMUNITY REPRESENTATION

Institutional ethics committees and Ministry of Health research-governance circulars emphasise participant welfare and accountability, but they rarely mandate structured community-level consultation for Indigenous research projects. As a result, protocols may satisfy administrative review criteria while overlooking socio-cultural implications.

The H3Africa governance model, analysed by Tindana et al. (2019), demonstrates how community advisory boards and participatory review structures can mitigate this gap. The ethical challenge in the Malaysian context based on the hypothetical scenario is therefore not absent of normative guidance but inconsistent operationalisation of participatory governance mechanisms.

(E) COMMERCIALISATION WITHOUT RECIPROCITY

The transformation of Indigenous genomic data into commercial ancestry algorithms intensifies ethical concern because it reinterprets communal heritage as a market commodity. Although this echoes commercialisation themes from Chapter 4, the distinctive element here is not profit alone but identity commodification. The absence of contractual provisions addressing indigenous intellectual or cultural rights reveals a structural vulnerability in Malaysian cross-border research governance when interfacing with global commercial actors.

International policy frameworks such as the OECD Recommendation (OECD, 2025) and standards articulated by Rehm et al. (2021) consistently emphasise benefit-sharing, transparency, and participatory engagement as safeguards against exploitative asymmetry. Their relevance lies in establishing normative convergence where statutory provisions remain silent.

Key Takeaways

- **Individual consent is insufficient where collective identity is implicated.**
  Malaysian research guidelines recognise respect for persons, yet Indigenous genomic research reveals that ethical legitimacy may require community-level consultation alongside individual authorisation. Biological data can function simultaneously as scientific resource and as cultural artefact.
- **Data protection does not equal cultural sovereignty.**
  The PDPA safeguards privacy and identifiability but does not address collective intellectual or cultural rights. Ethical governance must therefore extend beyond data security into recognition of group dignity and identity representation.
- **Benefit-sharing is a core component of justice, not a discretionary add-on.**
  The Code of Responsible Conduct in Research signals fairness and accountability as guiding principles. In Indigenous contexts, tangible reciprocity, such as health initiatives, education programmes, or shared intellectual recognition, functions as restorative justice rather than mere compensation.
- **Ethics committees require cultural literacy and community representation.**
  Oversight bodies play a critical anticipatory role, yet their effectiveness depends on inclusivity and contextual sensitivity. Participatory governance structures strengthen ethical foresight in cross-border Indigenous research.

- **Trust in Indigenous research is sustained through recognition, not procedural compliance.**
  International frameworks consistently emphasise cultural respect and participatory governance as foundations of legitimacy. Trust emerges when institutions demonstrate recognition of community sovereignty and identity, not merely adherence to anonymisation and consent formalities.

6.4.3 Case Study 3: Cross-Border Consent Breakdown

Case Narrative

A Malaysian public university enters into a collaborative oncology research agreement with a leading European cancer institute to investigate genetic markers associated with rare breast-cancer subtypes. The partnership is publicly celebrated as a milestone in international scientific cooperation, promising advanced sequencing technology, joint publications, and access to European research infrastructure.

Participants are recruited from public hospitals across several Malaysian states. Consent forms are drafted primarily in English, with brief verbal explanations provided in Bahasa Malaysia by overburdened clinical staff. No translated written versions are made available in Tamil, Mandarin, or Indigenous dialects. The consent language authorises "future cancer-related research collaborations" but does not specify potential downstream funding sources, cross-sector partnerships, or defence-linked biomedical projects abroad.

Several years later, participants discover through an online academic database that their samples were incorporated into a European defence-funded biomedical study examining radiation-exposure resilience. Although the research remains medically framed, its funding origin generates discomfort and mistrust among participants, some of whom object on ethical, religious, or political grounds. Community advocacy groups argue that participants were not adequately informed of potential downstream uses or the nature of foreign institutional partnerships.

The Malaysian university responds that the collaboration complied with institutional ethics approval and that all samples were coded and processed according to international standards. Nevertheless, the controversy exposes a deeper tension: linguistic limitations at the point of consent, gradual expansion of research scope over time, and the absence of ongoing communication channels between participants and the institution. The dilemma shifts from technical legality to cross-system legitimacy and accountability.

Commentary

(A) LINGUISTIC ADEQUACY AND THE MEANING OF CONSENT

The ethical fragility in this case begins with language rather than intent. Consent is not the mere presence of a signed document but the comprehension of implications. The Malaysian Guidelines on the Use of Human Biological Samples for Research (2nd ed.) emphasise that informed consent must be meaningful, culturally appropriate, and accessible to participants (Malaysia Ministry of Health, 2025). When consent forms are drafted in a language that is not fully understood by signers, ethical authorisation weakens even if procedural requirements are technically satisfied.

International scholarship on consent design for genomic data sharing, including the work by Riggs et al. (2019), demonstrates that linguistic accessibility and explanatory clarity are decisive factors in participant understanding of cross-border use. The issue here is not deception but structural inadequacy, whereby the participants were formally informed yet substantively under-informed.

(B) POST-CONSENT DRIFT AND MISSION CREEP

The expansion from civilian oncology research to defence-linked biomedical applications illustrates "mission creep", where consented purposes gradually evolve beyond their original framing. The scientific domain remained biomedical, but the change in funding source altered participants' moral interpretation of the research.

The Malaysian Code of Responsible Conduct in Research underscores integrity, transparency, and accountability in data stewardship, implying that substantial shifts in research direction warrant renewed ethical scrutiny or supplementary notification. As argued by Prictor et al. (2020) and Lay et al. (2025), static and one-time consent architectures are increasingly insufficient for long-term, data-intensive research ecosystems. Ethical governance therefore requires mechanisms for periodic consent review or participant notification, especially in cross-border collaborations with evolving institutional partners.

(C) LEGAL ASYMMETRY BETWEEN JURISDICTIONS

A central tension arises from asymmetry between Malaysian and European regulatory regimes. The Personal Data Protection Act 2010 (PDPA) provides foundational safeguards concerning confidentiality, consent, and cross-border transfer of identifiable personal data. However, once data are processed within European institutions governed by the GDPR, enforcement and participant recourse become jurisdictionally complex.

Scholarly work on re-identifiability of genomic data by Shabani and Marelli (2019) illustrates that even coded or pseudonymised datasets may fall within the scope of personal-data protection when re-identification remains technically plausible. Participants may paradoxically enjoy stronger formal privacy protections abroad while experiencing alienation due to unfamiliar legal systems and limited access to complaint mechanisms. Ethical governance must therefore evaluate not only legal adequacy but also perceived accessibility of justice.

(D) INSTITUTIONAL COMMUNICATION AND RELATIONAL ACCOUNTABILITY

The controversy reveals deficiencies in institutional communication infrastructure. Participants learned of the defence-funded project through external databases rather than by direct institutional engagement. An empirical study by Middleton et al. (2020) on global public perceptions of genomic data sharing demonstrates that willingness to participate is strongly correlated with perceptions of transparency and institutional responsiveness. Ethical legitimacy therefore depends on maintaining ongoing relational contact, not merely archival compliance.

Key Takeaways

- **Consent must be linguistically and culturally meaningful.**
  Malaysian research guidelines recognise accessibility and comprehension as integral to informed consent. Translation and culturally appropriate explanation are ethical prerequisites, not administrative courtesies, particularly in cross-border research where downstream implications may be complex.
- **Mission creep undermines expectation alignment.**
  The Code of Responsible Conduct in Research signals that integrity in stewardship includes transparency regarding evolving research scope. Periodic consent review or notification mechanisms help prevent post-consent drift from eroding participant trust.
- **Legal protection does not guarantee perceived justice.**
  The PDPA and foreign privacy regimes may offer technical safeguards, yet participants' sense of fairness depends on accessibility and familiarity of recourse mechanisms. Ethical legitimacy arises from perceived enforceability, not merely statutory adequacy.
- **Communication channels constitute ethical infrastructure.**
  Oversight frameworks and Ministry of Health governance instruments emphasise continuing accountability. Maintaining open communication transforms institutions from distant repositories into relational stewards of biological data.
- **Normative convergence is essential in transnational research.**
  International standards such as CIOMS, GA4GH frameworks, and OECD governance recommendations function as interpretive bridges where legal asymmetry exists. Ethical cross-border collaboration depends on aligning values and expectations, not solely on contractual or technical compliance.

6.5 Concluding Reflections

This chapter has demonstrated that international data sharing in biobanking is neither inherently exploitative nor automatically beneficial. Instead, it is an ethically contingent practice shaped by governance architecture, cultural sensitivity, and institutional accountability. The transnational movement of biological data magnifies the ethical tensions already present in domestic biobanking by introducing jurisdictional asymmetry, interpretive displacement, and unequal distributions of power and benefit. Cross-border collaboration therefore operates as a diagnostic lens through which the maturity of national research governance can be evaluated.

The three case studies collectively reveal that ethical fragility emerges not from collaboration but from misalignment between participant expectations and institutional action across borders. In the first case, broad consent language proved insufficient when data travelled beyond the jurisdictional and commercial contexts participants had reasonably imagined. In the second, individual authorisation failed to capture the collective cultural significance of Indigenous genomic identity, transforming a technical data transfer into a perceived act of symbolic dispossession. In the third, linguistic inadequacy and evolving research scope demonstrated how legal compliance in one system does not automatically translate into ethical legitimacy in another. Each scenario underscores that the central ethical risk in cross-border data sharing is not simply privacy breach but erosion of informational and cultural sovereignty.

Within the Malaysian regulatory landscape, a distinctive pattern becomes visible, whereby statutory and soft-law instruments provide robust procedural safeguards yet remain under-specified regarding collective rights, cross-border commercial partnerships, and community-level consent. The Personal Data Protection Act 2010 establishes foundational principles of confidentiality and cross-border transfer restrictions, but it does not fully address the relational or cultural dimensions of genomic data. The Malaysian Guidelines on the Use of Human Biological Samples for Research and the Code of Responsible Conduct in Research emphasise stewardship, transparency, and accountability, yet they function primarily as ethical compasses rather than as binding directives. Consequently, the governance of international data exchange relies heavily on institutional interpretation and ethics-committee deliberation, transforming oversight bodies into critical sites of normative reasoning rather than mere procedural checkpoints.

A recurring lesson throughout this chapter is that cross-border data sharing cannot be ethically sustained through contractual or technical safeguards alone. Encryption, anonymisation, and memoranda of understanding may protect data security, but they do not automatically preserve participant dignity, cultural recognition, or distributive fairness. Ethical sustainability requires what may be termed *normative convergence* – the deliberate alignment of values, expectations, and accountability mechanisms among collaborating institutions.

Such convergence does not demand uniform legal systems; instead, it demands shared ethical commitments to transparency, reciprocity, and cultural literacy.

The concept of sovereignty emerges as the chapter's unifying theme. Informational sovereignty concerns participants' ability to understand and influence the trajectories of their data. Cultural sovereignty pertains to communities' recognition and representation in how biological heritage is interpreted and utilised. Institutional sovereignty refers to the capacity of Malaysian research bodies to negotiate partnerships that preserve domestic ethical standards while engaging globally. These layers of sovereignty are interdependent; erosion in one dimension often reverberates across the others, manifesting as mistrust or disengagement from research participation.

From a policy perspective, the absence of a comprehensive statutory regime for cross-border genomic data sharing need not be interpreted solely as deficiency, as argued in the preceding chapters. Instead, it may be viewed as an opportunity for adaptive and participatory governance innovation. Harmonised institutional guidelines, explicit data-transfer registers, community consultation mechanisms, and benefit-sharing frameworks can provide substantive ethical safeguards without necessitating immediate legislative overhaul. Such measures shift governance from reactive compliance toward anticipatory stewardship, allowing institutions to respond flexibly to evolving scientific and geopolitical realities.

Ultimately, international collaboration in biobanking reveals that scientific progress and ethical responsibility are not competing imperatives but mutually reinforcing conditions. Participants contribute biological materials under implicit narratives of collective benefit and mutual respect. When cross-border partnerships operate transparently and reciprocally, they strengthen these narratives, expanding both knowledge and trust. When they operate opaquely or asymmetrically, they risk reproducing patterns of extraction that undermine the legitimacy of biomedical research.

The ethical sustainability of Malaysian biobanking in the international arena will therefore depend less on the perfection of regulatory instruments than on the cultivation of governance cultures that treat sovereignty, reciprocity, and accountability as relational commitments rather than legal afterthoughts. Cross-border data sharing, properly governed, becomes not a surrender of control but a collaborative extension of ethical stewardship, an affirmation that participation in global science need not come at the expense of local dignity or collective identity.

References

Abdul Aziz, M. F., & Mohd Yusof, A. N. (2019). Can dynamic consent facilitate the protection of biomedical big data in biobanking in Malaysia? *Asian Bioethics Review*, *11*(2), 209–222. https://pmc.ncbi.nlm.nih.gov/articles/PMC7747242/

Bull, S., Cheah, P. Y., Denny, S., Jao, I., Marsh, V., Merson, L., Shah More, N., Nhan L.N.T., Osrin, D., Tangseefa, D., Wassenaar, D., & Parker, M. (2015). Best practices for ethical sharing of individual-level health research data from low- and middle-income settings. *Journal of Empirical Research on Human Research Ethics*, *10*(3), 302–313. https://doi.org/10.1177/1556264615594606

Lawson, J., Cabili, M. N., Kerry, G., Boughtwood, T., Thorogood, A., Alper, P., Bowers, S. R., Boyles, R. R., Brookes, A. J., Brush, M., Burdett, T., Clissold, H., Donnelly, S., Dyke, S. O. M., Freeberg, M. A., Haendel, M. A., Hata, C., Holub, P., Jeanson, F.,. . . Courtot, M. (2021). The data use ontology to streamline responsible access to human biomedical datasets. *Cell Genomics*, *1*(2), 100028. https://doi.org/10.1016/j.xgen.2021.100028

Lay, W., Gasparini, L., Siero, W., & Hughes, E. K. (2025). A rapid review of the benefits and challenges of dynamic consent. *Research Ethics*, *21*(1), 180–202.

Malaysian Guidelines on the Use of Human Biological Samples for Research. (2025). Malaysia Ministry of Health.

Middleton, A., Milne, R., Almarri, M. A., Anwer, S., Atutornu, J., Baranova, E. E., Bevan, P., Cerezo, M., Cong, Y., Critchley, C., Fernow, J., Goodhand, P., Hasan, Q., Hibino, A., Houeland, G., Howard, H. C., Hussain, S. Z., Malmgren, C. I., Izhevskaya, V. L.,. . . Morley, K. I. (2020). Global public perceptions of genomic data sharing: What shapes the willingness to donate DNA and health data? *The American Journal of Human Genetics*, *107*(4), 743–752. https://doi.org/10.1016/j.ajhg.2020.08.023

Personal Data Protection Act. (2010).

Prictor, M., Lewis, M. A., Newson, A. J., Haas, M., Baba, S., Kim, H., Kokado, M., Minari, J., Molnár-Gábor, F., Yamamoto, B., Kaye, J., & Teare, H. J. A. (2020). Dynamic consent: An evaluation and reporting framework. *Journal of Empirical Research on Human Research Ethics*, *15*(3), 175–186. https://doi.org/10.1177/1556264619887073

Recommendation of the Council on Enhancing Access to and Sharing of Data. (2025). OECD. https://legalinstruments.oecd.org/en/instruments/OECD-LEGAL-0463

Rehm, H. L., Page, A. J. H., Smith, L., Adams, J. B., Alterovitz, G., Babb, L. J., Barkley, M. P., Baudis, M., Beauvais, M. J. S., Beck, T., Beckmann, J. S., Beltran, S., Bernick, D., Bernier, A., Bonfield, J. K., Boughtwood, T. F., Bourque, G., Bowers, S. R., Brookes, A. J.,. . . Birney, E. (2021). GA4GH: International policies and standards for data sharing across genomic research and healthcare. *Cell Genomics*, *1*(2), 100029. https://doi.org/10.1016/j.xgen.2021.100029

Riggs, E. R., Azzariti, D. R., Niehaus, A., Goehringer, S. R., Ramos, E. M., Rodriguez, L. L., Knoppers, B., Rehm, H. L., & Martin, C. L. (2019). Development of a consent resource for genomic data sharing in the clinical setting. *Genetics in Medicine*, *21*(1), 81–88. https://doi.org/10.1038/s41436-018-0017-5

Shabani, M., & Marelli, L. (2019). Re-identifiability of genomic data and the GDPR. *The EMBO Reports*, *20*(6), EMBR201948316. https://doi.org/10.15252/embr.201948316

Sirugo, G., Williams, S. M., & Tishkoff, S. A. (2019). The missing diversity in human genetic studies. *Cell*, *177*(1), 26–31. https://doi.org/10.1016/j.cell.2019.02.048

Tindana, P., Yakubu, A., Staunton, C., Matimba, A., Littler, K., Madden, E., Munung, N. S., & de Vries, J. (2019). Engaging research ethics committees to develop an ethics and governance framework for best practices in genomic research and biobanking in Africa: The H3Africa model. *BMC Medical Ethics*, *20*(1), 69. https://doi.org/10.1186/s12910-019-0398-2

7 Concluding Thoughts

Towards Relational and Responsible Biobank Governance in Malaysia

7.1 Revisiting the Promise and the Paradox of Biobanking

Biobanks have emerged as indispensable infrastructures in contemporary biomedical science. Throughout this book, they have been described not merely as storage facilities for biological samples but as dynamic research platforms that enable population-level studies, precision medicine, and translational innovation. In the Malaysian context, biobanks hold particular significance because of the country's ethnic, cultural, and genetic diversity, which provides a uniquely rich foundation for scientific discovery and regional collaboration. The promise of biobanking, therefore, lies in its capacity to generate knowledge that improves public-health outcomes, strengthens research capacity, and positions Malaysia within global biomedical networks.

Yet this promise is accompanied by a persistent paradox. The very features that make biobanks scientifically valuable given its large-scale data aggregation, long-term storage, and international interoperability, also generate ethical and legal complexity. As this book has argued from its opening chapters, technological progress in biobanking frequently advances more rapidly than the regulatory and ethical frameworks designed to govern it do. The challenge is not whether biobanks should exist. The challenge is how they should be governed so that scientific advancement does not outpace moral responsibility.

7.2 Converging Ethical Themes Across the Book

The preceding chapters have examined a spectrum of ethical and legal dilemmas arising from biobank governance in Malaysia. Each chapter addressed a distinct issue – namely, consent, privacy, commercialisation, incidental findings, and cross-border data sharing – but these concerns are not isolated developments. Rather, they reveal recurring normative patterns centred on value, control, and trust.

The discussion of consent in Chapter 2 highlighted autonomy not as a single moment of signature but as a continuing process of understanding and

DOI: 10.4324/9781003745785-7

communication. Privacy and confidentiality, explored in Chapter 3, extended this concern into the informational domain, demonstrating that protection of data is inseparable from protection of dignity. Commercialisation introduced the economic dimension of value, raising questions about fairness, benefit-sharing, and the legitimacy of profit derived from human biological materials. The governance of incidental findings examined the clinical and informational value of knowledge itself, questioning whether silence or disclosure better serves participant welfare. Finally, cross-border data sharing illuminated the sovereign and geopolitical dimensions of biobank governance, exposing tensions between openness and cultural control.

Overall, these themes demonstrate that biobank governance is fundamentally concerned with different forms of value attached to human biological materials, such as moral, informational, economic, clinical, and sovereignty. Ethical dilemmas emerge when these values intersect without adequate frameworks to mediate them. What appears as distinct challenges across chapters ultimately converges into a shared question: how can institutions manage biological resources in a manner that respects both individual rights and collective interests? This question has remained constant, even as the contexts shift.

7.3 Trust as the Invisible Infrastructure

A central insight that emerges across all chapters is the role of trust as the invisible yet indispensable infrastructure of biobanking. Participants contribute biological samples not solely because of legal assurances but because of an implicit belief that institutions will act responsibly, transparently, and fairly. Trust enables participation. Trust sustains long-term engagement. Without it, even the most technically sophisticated governance framework risks becoming ineffective.

It can be argued that trust is not purely contractual or legalistic. It is relational and communal. It is shaped by cultural values, religious sensitivities, and collective experiences with public institutions. Biobank governance, therefore, cannot rely exclusively on statutory compliance or technical safeguards. It must also cultivate relational accountability through transparent communication, meaningful consent processes, and visible stewardship. Trust is not secured through perfection of outcomes but through coherence of process, whereby participants must perceive that decisions are guided by fairness rather than convenience. This perception, once lost, is difficult to rebuild.

7.4 From Compliance to Stewardship

One of the recurring lessons of this book is the need to move beyond a compliance-oriented approach toward a stewardship-based model of governance. Whereas compliance emphasises adherence to rules and procedural checklists, stewardship emphasises ongoing responsibility, ethical reflexivity, and anticipatory governance. The distinction is subtle, but its implications are significant.

In biobanking, this shift matters because the implications of research often extend far beyond the moment of sample collection. Stewardship involves recognising that biological materials represent enduring relationships between participants and institutions rather than one-time transactions. Dynamic consent mechanisms, periodic policy review, ethics-committee deliberation, and community engagement initiatives exemplify stewardship in practice. These mechanisms transform governance from a reactive system, addressing problems only after they arise, into a proactive culture capable of anticipating ethical risks and responding adaptively. The emphasis is not on rigid control but on responsible custodianship grounded in transparency, inclusivity, and respect.

7.5 Malaysia's Governance Trajectory: Fragmented But Adaptive

Malaysia's biobank governance framework, as analysed in earlier chapters, is characterised by fragmentation across statutes, guidelines, and institutional practices. It would be misleading to describe this landscape simply as inadequate. A more accurate characterisation is that it is evolving. The absence of a dedicated biobank law presents challenges, but it also reflects an environment in which soft-law instruments, professional codes, and ethics committees exercise meaningful influence. Ethical oversight emerges through institutional collaboration and normative dialogue rather than solely through legislative mandate.

This adaptive trajectory presents both constraints and opportunities. Harmonisation of guidelines, clearer coordination among oversight bodies, and increased community representation could strengthen coherence without sacrificing flexibility. Malaysia's multicultural and multi-religious context positions it uniquely to contribute to regional discourse on ethical biobanking, potentially serving as a model for culturally sensitive governance within Southeast Asia. The path forward, therefore, lies not in wholesale regulatory overhaul but in incremental convergence toward shared principles of accountability, reciprocity, and transparency.

7.6 Final Reflections: Biobanks as Repositories of Relationships

The concluding insight of this book is that biobanks should be understood not merely as repositories of biological samples or data but as repositories of relationships. Each stored specimen represents a connection between participant and institution, between individual identity and collective scientific endeavour, and between present research and future societal benefit. Ethical governance must therefore protect not only information but also the relational trust that sustains participation across time.

Biobanks succeed ethically when participants feel respected, informed, and fairly treated, even years after their initial contribution. This requires governance cultures that recognise biological materials as extensions of personhood and community identity rather than as abstract research assets. Ultimately, the ethical sustainability of Malaysian biobanking depends less on the existence of rigid statutory mandates than on the cultivation of relational governance grounded in dignity, cultural literacy, and institutional accountability.

Scientific progress and ethical responsibility need not be opposing forces. When guided by trust and transparency, they become mutually reinforcing pillars of a research ecosystem that honours both knowledge and humanity.

Index

For Product Safety Concerns and Information please contact our EU representative GPSR@taylorandfrancis.com Taylor & Francis Verlag GmbH, Kaufingerstraße 24, 80331 München, Germany